San Francisco Lightship, Number 83, *marked the entrance to the Golden Gate for two decades. She was moored just west of the San Francisco bar, a position the ship had to maintain during the most severe conditions. (U.S. Coast Guard)*

LIGHTHOUSES AND LIFEBOATS
on the
REDWOOD COAST

Ralph C. Shanks, Jr.
and
Janetta Thompson Shanks

COSTAÑO BOOKS   BOX 791   SAN ANSELMO, CALIFORNIA

COSTAÑO BOOKS
P.O. BOX 791
SAN ANSELMO, CALIFORNIA 94960

By the same authors:
Lighthouses of San Francisco Bay

Library of Congress Catalog Card Number 77-93457

ISNB 0-930268-04-0 (Hardcover edition)
ISNB 0-930268-03-2 (Softcover edition)

DEDICATED TO:

Wayne R. Piland, U.S. Lighthouse Service
William Owens, U.S. Lighthouse Service
J. Milford Johnson, U.S. Lighthouse Service
Garner Churchill, U.S. Coast Guard

Ye have to go out —
—but ye don't have to come in.

Traditional Motto of the Surfmen

Punta Gorda
Donald Lacewell Shanks

LIGHTHOUSES AND LIFEBOATS

ON THE

REDWOOD COAST

TABLE OF CONTENTS

* * *

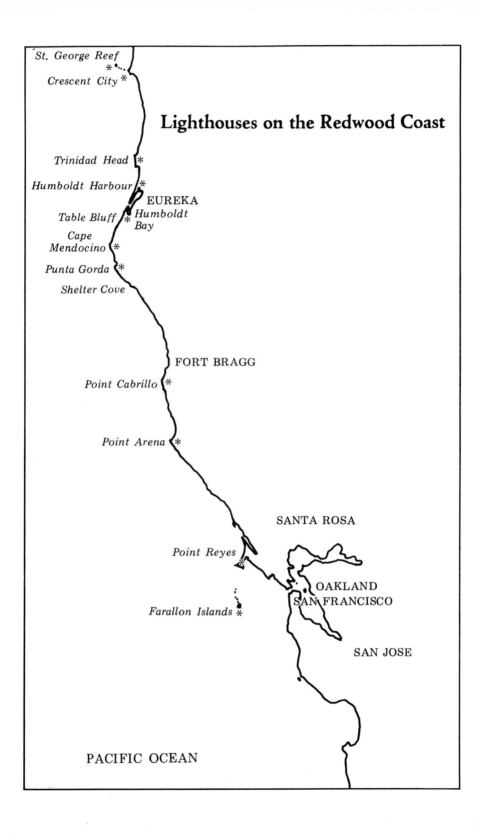

Lighthouses on the Redwood Coast

St. George Reef *
Crescent City *

Trinidad Head *
Humboldt Harbour *
EUREKA
Table Bluff * Humboldt
Bay
Cape
Mendocino *
Punta Gorda *
Shelter Cove

FORT BRAGG
Point Cabrillo *

Point Arena *

SANTA ROSA

Point Reyes

OAKLAND
SAN FRANCISCO
Farallon Islands *

SAN JOSE

PACIFIC OCEAN

INTRODUCTION

California's Redwood Coast extends from the Golden Gate to the Oregon border. For over three hundred miles the shore is lonely, wild, and dangerous. Here, the mariner must contend with the heaviest fog on the Pacific coast, the possibility of storm waves exceeding one hundred feet in height, and gales bringing winds of over one hundred miles per hour and lasting days and even weeks at a time.

The Redwood Coast does not offer an open-handed welcome to the mariner. It is a coastline with few harbors and little shelter. A ship on the Redwood Coast must set a long course when sailing from one isolated harbor to another, and refuge may be fifty or seventy-five miles away. The few ports are almost always ringed by heavy, often impassable surf. Offshore rocks are frequently hidden hazards. As towering bluffs finally give way to a new port, the mariner may have to steer his craft across a treacherous bar, a task which becomes impossible in heavy weather.

The survival of California's north coastal economy has long depended upon developing reliable and safe sea routes. Given the unusual hazards mariners encountered, coupled with the region's heavy dependence upon shipping to reach the nation's markets, establishing a chain of lighthouses, lightships, and buoys became a high priority for early-day coastal communities. San Francisco, Eureka, Crescent City, and Trinidad—among others—all were demanding lighthouses by the 1850's. As a result, lighthouses became the first chain of coastal buildings to dot northern California's shore from San Francisco to Oregon.

The strong winds, heavy rains (up to 150 inches annually), rugged terrain, huge waves, and extreme isolation of the Redwood Coast dictated that the light stations established there must be among the finest in America. Built at the extremities of North America's most exposed points, these lighthouses had to withstand incredible forces which also included earthquakes, tornadoes, floods, landslides, inundating tides, and even occasional snowstorms. Many of the light stations were so isolated that contact with the outside world came just four times a year. The light keepers and their families responded by becoming an unusually self-sufficient breed, skilled at many tasks. All of these skills combined to accomplish two principal goals: to keep the light and fog signal functioning, and to assure the survival of the light-keeping families. To fail at either task meant disaster.

Construction of a fine chain of lighthouses did not mean an end to shipwrecks on the Redwood Coast. In 1878 the U.S. Life-Saving Service began building another chain of stations to aid mariners. These were the

The powerful beams of Point Arena lighthouse's first order lens shine with the intensity of 1,200,000 candle power and can be seen for 19 miles out to sea. (Bill and Isabel Owens)

life-saving stations, designed not to prevent marine disasters but to assist where wrecks had already occurred. Equipped with self-bailing, self-righting lifeboats and with surfboats, line-throwing Lyle guns, breeches buoys, and a myriad of other rescue apparatus, the crews (called surfmen) of the life-saving stations added greatly to the odds of a shipwreck victim surviving on this rugged coast. Like the lighthouses, life-saving stations were established at a number of particularly dangerous locations. The exciting story of the life-saving stations is interwoven with the history of the lighthouses.

Last to arrive were the lightships. Sometimes called floating lighthouses, these little vessels marked the most turbulent waters on the west coast. Operated by the U.S. Lighthouse Service and later by the Coast Guard, the lightship crews underwent amazing hardships as they stood what has been termed the most dangerous duty in the Coast Guard.

Operation and Organization

From 1852 until 1939 all of California's lighthouses and lightships were under the jurisdiction of the U.S. Lighthouse Service, a branch of the Federal government. The Lighthouse Service was organized into districts, all of them under a central Board in Washington, D.C. Each district was under the charge of a lighthouse inspector and his office staff. The districts all had one or more supply depots equipped with supply ships called lighthouse tenders. The lighthouse tenders made regular calls at each light station and lightship in their district, bringing almost every possible item the station's keepers required. Such visits generally occurred four times a year and often coincided with an inspection by district officials.

All of California's lighthouses were in the 12th (later, in 1910, renumbered the 18th) Lighthouse District, with headquarters in the old Customs House in San Francisco. While some unlighted buoys and other supplies were kept at small "buoy depots" at Los Angeles Harbor, San Diego's Ballast Point, and on Humboldt Bay's North Spit, the 12th District's main supply depot for California'a lighthouses, lightships, and lighted buoys was on San Francisco Bay's Yerba Buena Island. Pier 15 in San Francisco supplemented the island lighthouse depot as a facility for loading tenders.

The light stations were staffed with from one to five attendants, called keepers. The light required constant attention, since its light source was either an oil lamp or, later, an incandescent oil vapor lamp, both of which required frequent adjustments and fueling. Keepers at stations with fog signals had additional burdens when these were in operation. Some fog signals were steam-powered whistles or sirens, and operating such equipment was so strenuous that such stations seldom had less than four keepers. By contrast, lighthouses with no fog signal or those having only a bell usually were manned by but one or two attendants.

For the benefit of readers unfamiliar with lighthouse operation, we will quote a passage from our earlier book, *Lighthouses of San Francisco Bay*, which contains a concise explanation of lighthouse equipment and functions. It begins by describing the first lenses developed by the French genius, Augustine Fresnel, and used to light California's beacons:

The new Fresnel lenses were magnificent. They were composed of hand-ground glass prisms and glass "bull's eyes" mounted in a gleaming brass framework. On large lenses there were over 1,000 individual pieces of glass, and at night all the lenses gave the appearance of gigantic, glistening diamonds. An oil lamp was placed inside the lens, using a glass chimney to carry smoke up to a ball-shaped opening on the lighthouse roof. At night, the lamp was lighted, its diverse rays being focused into powerful beams by the refracting character of the prisms. The Fresnel lenses were so efficient at focusing the lamp rays that beams could often be seen for over 20 miles at sea.

For some lighthouses, an immovable fixed lens with a steady light beam was sufficient to warn mariners. But for others, some sort of flashing pattern had to be created so that there could be no question as to which lighthouse was in sight. To create a flashing effect the entire lens was placed on wheels or ball bearings which ran in a track at the base of the lens. A clockwork drive, powered by a weight, was used to rotate the lens. Several times a night, keepers would rewind the weight to keep the lens turning. Such flashing lenses had their prisms and bull's eyes arranged in panels. As the lens turned, light beams showed steadily from each panel, but to the mariner at sea the light appeared to be flashing. The effect was created because each time the panel lined up with a viewer, the viewer could see a flash of light, but in between the panels the light appeared to go dark. It was an ingenious device and it is still in use today.

Gleaming third order lens awaits installation at Point Cabrillo lighthouse on the Mendocino coast. These flash panels with bull's eyes provided a brilliant white flash once every ten seconds as the entire glass portion rotated. C. 1909. (U.S. Coast Guard)

Lighthouse and buoy lenses were repaired in the "lamp house" at the Lighthouse Service Depot on Yerba Buena Island between San Francisco and Oakland. C. 1930's. (U.S. Coast Guard)

Fresnel classified his lenses by order, the largest being of the first order and the smallest of the sixth order. The following chart indicates their approximate size.

Order	Height	Inside Diameter
First	7' 10"	6' 1"
Second	6' 1"	4' 7"
Third	4' 8"	3' 3"
Fourth	2' 4"	1' 8"
Fifth	1' 8"	1' 3"
Sixth	1' 5"	1' 0"

Large first or second order lenses were used primarily at coastal lights where it was important for the light to be seen from many miles out to sea. Smaller-order lenses were used most often in harbors. . . .

In addition to a light, most California lighthouses had a fog signal. The fog signal might be a whistle, a horn, a bell, a siren,

Coquille River (Bandon, Oregon) Life-Saving Station's crew pose with their pulling lifeboat. To the left of the lifeboat can be seen the line-throwing Lyle gun and the rectangular faking box. C. pre-1915. (San Francisco Maritime Museum)

With the surf running high and the bar breaking, the Life-Saving Service crew at Coquille River Station holds its weekly "boat drill." Such drills were held even on extremely rough days, often drawing large crowds of onlookers. C. pre-1915. (San Francisco Maritime Museum)

or even a cannon. All fog signals had the common feature of emitting a patterned sound warning during foggy weather. Light lists also included fog signal characteristics; and just as mariners could identify a lighthouse by its flashing characteristic, they could also recognize it by the number, duration, or frequency of blasts emitted by the fog signal. . . .

Lighthouses also aided the mariner on clear days. For those unfamiliar with the coast, early light lists often included illustrations of light stations to aid in identification. The distinctively-shaped lighthouse provided unquestionable confirmation of a ship's position.

Today, modern lighthouses also aid the seaman by means of a radio beacon, a device which, like lights and fog signals, sends a repetitive signal by which mariners can fix their position. Thus, lighthouses now broadcast their warnings using radio waves as well as light and sound waves.

In 1939, as an economy move by the Roosevelt administration, the Lighthouse Service was absorbed by the U.S. Coast Guard. Today, most of the state's lighthouses are still under the jurisdiction of the Coast Guard's Aids to Navigation Branch in San Francisco. All the beacons save one, Marin County's Point Bonita light station, have been converted to automatic operation and are unmanned.

The U.S. Life-Saving Service was organized similarly to the Lighthouse Service. Headquartered in Washington, D.C., it too divided the United States into districts. Its largest district was on the Pacific coast and comprised California, Oregon, Washington, and Alaska. Most life-saving stations had a keeper (the officer in charge) and a crew of between six and eight surfmen. The keeper directed most rescues, ran the station, and trained his crews. During the early days, the stations were equipped only with pulling boats and carts that had to be hauled over the sands by the men themselves.

The Life-Saving Service was a civilian organization, operating in California from 1878 until 1915. At that time it was merged with the Revenue Cutter Service to create the modern Coast Guard. In this book we will refer to the "life-saving" stations before 1915 and to "lifeboat" stations after 1915 as they became referred to by the Coast Guard.

While just one of the Life-Saving Service's original stations remains in use today (Fort Point Coast Guard Station in San Francisco), its earliest buildings were replaced by architecturally similar buildings constructed by the Coast Guard between 1915 and 1937. One of these Coast Guard stations, Humboldt Bay, is still active, and it carries on many of the Life-Saving Service's traditional operations.

The lighthouses, life-saving stations, and lightships all offer a fascinating glimpse into California's maritime history. The authors have

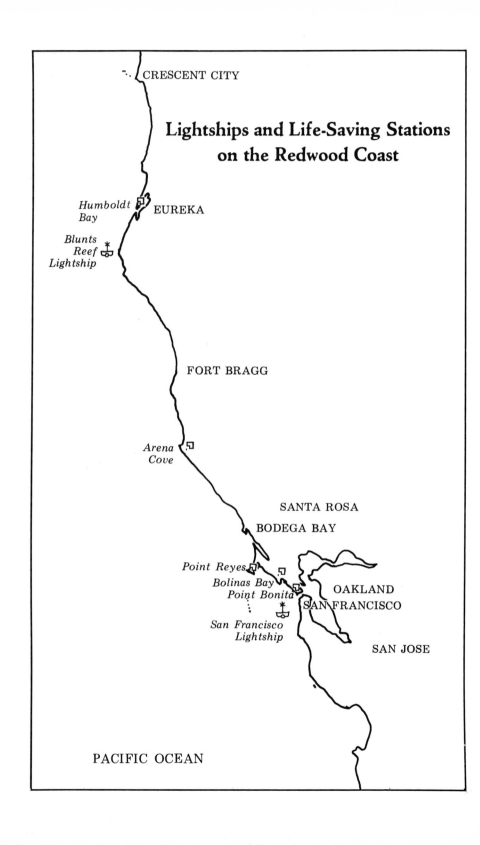

CRESCENT CITY

**Lightships and Life-Saving Stations
on the Redwood Coast**

*Humboldt
Bay*   EUREKA

*Blunts
Reef
Lightship*

FORT BRAGG

*Arena
Cove*

SANTA ROSA

BODEGA BAY

Point Reyes

*Bolinas Bay
Point Bonita*   OAKLAND

SAN FRANCISCO

*San Francisco
Lightship*

SAN JOSE

PACIFIC OCEAN

spent nearly a decade interviewing retired light keepers and surfmen and their families. Nearly all of those who supplied information for our book were in their seventies, eighties, or nineties. All had experienced exciting events along the mist-shrouded Redwood Coast. We have attempted to provide a maritime history which vividly and accurately details the lives of an important segment of our coastal people.

Join us now as we climb the iron stairways of the Redwood Coast's sentinels and relight the ancient wicks. There are watches to be stood and beaches to patrol. There are many stories to be told and, perhaps, at the end of our voyage a course will have been charted so that we can preserve the lighthouses and lifeboat stations for those yet to see California's Redwood Coast.

. . .

For those unfamiliar with maritime terminology, a glossary has been included at the end of the book. All locations are in California unless otherwise stated.

Point Reyes Life-Saving Station's beach patrolmen leave their footprints in the sand as they pass the wreckage of the steam schooner Samoa, *which was lost in 1913. (Howard Underhill)*

POINT REYES AND BOLINAS BAY

The Point Reyes peninsula curves sharply seaward for ten miles. Much of it is low and difficult to see from offshore; although its very tip is high, soaring over six hundred feet above the Pacific and appearing like an island from the sea. For nine months of the year the region is often cloaked in thick fog, for this is the foggiest point on the Pacific Coast and probably in all America. It is the nation's windiest headland as well, and the incessant northwesterlies sometimes blow at over 130 miles per hour. Offshore, the ocean currents become confusing, moving in opposite directions. The sea is deep, too, so that the early-day mariner could not use a lead line to determine his depth or position. A breaking beach and rocks often loom without warning. Worse, configurations in the headlands and other causes make it difficult to hear the warning blast of a fog horn when vessels approach from the north. Stranding was a terrible prospect for Point Reyes beach may well have the heaviest surf in California. Here, then, is a fitting graveyard for ships.

The whole history of California maritime disasters began here when, in 1595, the *San Augustin* became California's first shipwreck. In subsequent years, at least sixty more vessels would be lost from Duxbury Reef north to Bodega Bay.

Because of its dangers, Point Reyes was chosen as one of the original West Coast lighthouse sites; and Congressional funds were approved just two years after California achieved statehood. Land on the windswept point was, at that time, selling for but a few dollars an acre and the government needed only a small parcel. Some $25,000 was authorized to buy the land and build the light station. When government agents approached the parcel's owners, however, they were stunned to discover that the price of the land had suddenly been raised to . . . $25,000. The Federal government refused to pay such an outlandish price, and the headland remained unmarked for seventeen more years. During that period, there were at least fourteen shipwrecks, some of which undoubtedly would have been prevented by a lighthouse. When the land was finally obtained in 1869, the government paid but $6,000 and received 120 acres. Along with the lighthouse reservation, a landing site was purchased on Drake's Bay (near today's Fish Docks) and a right-of-way linking the two parcels was granted. By 1870 con-

Point Reyes lighthouse keeper Tom Smith engages in the centuries-old task of cleaning salt spray from the lantern room windows. Inside is the magnificent first order lens with over 1,000 pieces of hand-ground glass. 1975 (R. Shanks)

Point Reyes light station clings to the spine of a headland hundreds of feet high. Lowest structure is the original fog signal building. Midway up the cliff can be seen the lighthouse and powerhouse, while the weather station occupies the very summit. Dwellings and support buildings are landward of the weather station. C. 1933. (U.S. Coast Guard)

struction materials were landed on Drake's Bay, and men and materials came ashore at the newly-built wharf and storage shed.

Construction superintendent was to be Phineas F. Marston, a Maine man, who had begun his career building New England churches. Marston had come west by the Panama route. Arriving in San Francisco with his wife and four children, he was hired by a friend to construct Army barracks at the Presidio, Angel Island, and Black Point. His work was good, and upon completion of the barracks, Colonel R. S. Williams, lighthouse engineer, hired him as superintendent of construction for the Lighthouse Service. Marston was first sent to the Pacific Northwest with his initial assignment to build Ediz Hook light in Washington. Before his work was finished, his wife died. Despite the tragedy, he completed the project. He returned to California in 1867 with a new bride and a new set of stations to be built. His first assignment—to build Point Reyes lighthouse and fog signal.

Small, house-like structure at lower left is the original fog signal building. The nearly vertical coal chute and adjacent trail illustrate the steep climb keepers faced daily. Winds here sometimes surpassed 130 miles per hour. C. 1880. (Bancroft Library)

Work began with wagons carrying materials over two miles of steep hills from the landing to the top of the headland. By now lighthouse engineers had learned that California's fog is often high-altitude fog and that a beacon must be placed well down the side of a headland where there is less fog. At Point Reyes two terraces had to be carved from solid rock, one about one hundred feet above the sea for the fog signal and the other at an elevation of about two hundred fifty feet for the lighthouse. Both sites were on sheer cliffs covered with fine rocks that made keeping one's footing very difficult, especially when high winds buffeted the point. If any of the construction workers lost his footing, there would be little chance of surviving a fall.

A combination stairway and coal chute was built from the top of the headland down to both sites. A little flatcar with a bulkhead at the lower end was designed to run up and down the chute, drawn by a cable powered by a winch at the head of the stairs. The stairs and the chute were both impressive. The stairs to the lighthouse numbered an exhausting 300 steps, while to reach the fog signal at its lower site required an incredible 638 steps. The chute could boast some sections where it dropped down at an incline of well over 50 degrees.

In order to combat the high winds, the lighthouse was forged of iron plate and literally bolted to the cliff. The tower was sixteen-sided, possessed two balconies, and was painted white with a large, black lantern room to hold its first order lens. The lens installed was one of the most beautiful ever built by the Paris firm of Barbier and Fenestre. It boasted 24 panels, over 1,000 hand-ground prisms, and was mounted in gleaming brass. The lens produced a flash once every five seconds.

The light tower was considered by some to be the finest iron-plate lighthouse in the United States, and Marston and his fellows must have been pleased. Marston was to go on from this triumph to build majestic Pigeon Point lighthouse in San Mateo County. He would cap his career by constructing the fog signal stations at Año Nuevo Island and at Point Montara. He had gained invaluable experience for working on the latter two stations when he built the frame fog signal building at Point Reyes.

Marston's crew had built one other noteworthy structure at Point Reyes. This was the spacious, two-story, frame dwelling which would house the four keepers and their families. Nearby, a huge cistern was completed to supply water for both domestic use and for the fog signal's boilers. A rancher was contracted with to deliver firewood, coal, oil, and—if the cistern ran dry—water.

On December 1, 1870, the keepers lighted the lamp and started up the fog signal. There was the Principal or Head Keeper, referred to in the custom of the Lighthouse Service simply as "Keeper." His assistants were called, according to rank, First Assistant, Second Assistant, and Third Assistant. Frequently the term "Assistant" was dropped, so that

The heart of Point Reyes Light Station was this cluster of buildings. Alongside the lighthouse stands the powerhouse containing generators, air compressors, and air tank for the fog signal below. The small concrete building at left is the oil house. 1941. (U.S. Coast Guard)

The original dwelling was an impressive structure. Two lesser houses were built opposite this duplex to provide additional living quarters. C. 1940's. (U.S. Coast Guard)

a keeper might say, "I was First at Point Reyes after beginning my career years ago as Third at St. George Reef."

Those initial two decades at Point Reyes were not to be glorious ones for the light station. They were, rather, years of annoying difficulties, disasters, and even tragedy. In 1872 the new fog signal building burned to the ground. The following July, in the middle of the foggiest season, the newly rebuilt steam fog signal ran out of water and stopped sounding. Even when it was working, the fog signal consumed 140 pounds of coal an hour, and every sack of it had to be carefully lowered down the coal chute. Then, despite the fact that the navigational aids were finally operating smoothly, the *Warrior Queen* ran ashore in thick fog on July 19, 1874. The next day second assistant E. K. Lincoln went down to visit the wreck. A high surf was running and Lincoln disappeared, presumably drowning. A year later an Italian fishing boat grounded nearby. The keepers rushed to help. This time it was not a wickie who mysteriously disappeared. When principal keeper John C. Bull and his men arrived, they found a crewless boat.

John Bull had been good for Point Reyes. Under his leadership, the station had functioned well, and the crew had apparently had amicable relations. To be sure, the lens wheels had become worn, but Bull simply jacked up the lens, used some wedges to tilt it, and installed ten new chariot wheels. Then, in August, 1875, Bull was replaced by a new principal keeper, and Point Reyes was headed for trouble.

The new keeper immediately found his assistants uncontrollable. The third assistant did not bother to start the fog signal until two hours after the fog rolled in, an inexcusable oversight. Further, the third assistant informed his new boss that he "refused to work over one-half day for any man in the Lighthouse Service." Soon both the second and third assistants were refusing to go on duty a half-hour before sunset (official Lighthouse Service practice was to get the lamps ready before dark), informing the new head keeper that beginning work after sundown was quite soon enough.

The third assistant seems to have been the least dedicated. He next delayed starting the fog signal for 2½ hours after the fog had arrived. When the crew went looking for him, he was nowhere to be found! Even when he did show up for watch at the fog signal, he only blew the whistle at his leisure. Instead of sounding the whistle once a minute as required, the third assistant felt that a blast once every five to fifteen minutes was sufficient. Worse, he did not bother to build up much steam and his infrequent toots were none too loud. Later on in the year the incorrigible assistant keeper further curtailed his duties by not bothering to blow the whistle at all during thick weather. A month later, he started disappearing from the station, sometimes for an entire night at a time. Having him on watch was almost worse than having him absent.

He began tinkering with the equipment, readjusting the "bell" in the whistle, a serious step since the position of the whistle's bell determined the quality of its sound and hence its effectiveness.

Three days later there was more trouble. The rope which pulled the handcart up the chute suddenly snapped. The car shot down the chute at "violent speed" and crashed through a shed and into the lighthouse sleeping room. The lackadaisical attitudes had finally paid off—nobody was at the lighthouse and thus no one was injured. The cart and shed were badly damaged.

December, 1875, began with the theft of high-quality lens cleaning towels. No one was accused, but the head keeper had his suspicions; the troublesome third assistant was given notice of dismissal. Trouble continued into the new year. The tender *Shubrick* arrived at Drake's Bay with the lighthouse inspector on board. After reading the station log and talking with the keepers, he must have returned to his ship with a stunned expression on his face. The *Shubrick* delivered supplies and

Illustrating common Lighthouse Service practice during the 1920's and 1930's, a gasoline launch tows a whaleboat loaded with empty gas and oil drums back to tender Sequoia. *Oil, gas, and coal came ashore at Drake's Bay and was then hauled overland to the light station. Empty drums and coal sacks were returned to the ship to arrive refilled on the tender's next visit months later. 1922. (U.S. Coast Guard)*

picked up empty oil drums and coal bags; she then steamed off for the Farallon Islands. Back at the lighthouse, a gale promptly came up and blew so hard that all the station's fences were flattened.

The third assistant finally left in late January, 1876. The head keeper then turned his attention to his first assistant. The first assistant had by now become "a grumbling nuisance," who spilled oil on clean wicks, failed to carry out orders, and was slow in starting the fog whistle. The Lighthouse Service had had enough. In July one L. Middleton arrived. He had orders to dismiss the dissatisfied head keeper and assume his duties. Once this was accomplished, his first action was taken immediately. He fired the two remaining assistant keepers and started with a fresh crew.

The new men seemed to work out well, but Point Reyes was a hard station, and it continued to take its toll. One of the assistants soon resigned, saying the work was "too heavy." Middleton may have agreed, for he too resigned shortly afterwards.

When the inspector returned in February, 1877 the constant turnover and conflict had allowed things to be "in anything but a creditable condition, showing in many cases want of care and attention."

The fledgling light station was having its troubles, but down at Bolinas Bay conditions would become even worse. The Point Reyes region continued to be the scene of shipwrecks. By 1881 the U.S. Life-Saving Service had established a life-saving station on Bolinas Bay. The southern approaches to Point Reyes were particularly dangerous, especially at Duxbury Reef; and a manned and well-equipped rescue station could be a blessing whenever a shipwreck occurred. Unfortunately, the life-saving station was neither well-equipped nor well-manned. A keeper was hired; but whenever a shipwreck occurred, he was expected to round up a volunteer crew to man the surfboat. This proved even more frustrating than trying to operate Point Reyes lighthouse. Then, on April 15, 1885, after only four years of operation, the station caught fire. There was a strong northwest wind blowing and inside the station were ten pounds of powder for the Lyle gun. With the gunpowder inside, nobody volunteered to get very close to fight the fire. The station burned to the ground.

As if that were not enough, the cause turned out to be arson and the indicted arsonist the station keeper. Fortunately, for his sake, the poor keeper was never convicted. However, the station was not to be rebuilt until 1915. For the thirty intervening years, the crews of ships stranding on dangerous Duxbury Reef could expect little in the way of assistance.

While the manpower problems at the lighthouse seemed to have been solved, the fog problem had no solution. The fog was of unparalleled duration. A new steam siren had replaced the old whistle. To fuel

Powerful "super typhon," compressed air fog horns could often be heard for five miles out to sea; at other times they were inaudible a short distance to the north of Point Reyes. 1975. (R. Shanks)

it, wagonloads of 100 to 120 sacks of coal would be brought up from the landing. It was common for over eighty tons of coal to be burned annually. On one occasion the fog signal blasted away, non-stop, for eight days. Worse yet was the time a *San Francisco Chronicle* reporter visited the station. He found that "the sirens had been in operation for 176 consecutive hours and the jaded attendants looked as if they had been on a protracted spree."

The wind, too, was a constant harassment. The roof was literally blown off the dwelling, shutters were smashed, chimneys blown down, and fences flattened. During windstorms, salt spray was carried over three hundred feet into the air, coating the lighthouse windows and reducing the effectiveness of the light. The keepers then had to climb up on the light tower and clean the windows periodically throughout the night. During particularly violent storms the thick window panes in the lantern room were blown out; the wickies had to keep large brass clamps on hand to hold emergency panels in place when such breakage occurred.

Rain was another elemental hazard. On September 14, 1888, it rained so hard that the water in the cistern rose two feet during the night. When John C. Ryan assumed the post of principal keeper in 1888, he found that the wind and rain had left the station looking more like "an old lumber mill," and despite some valiant efforts by his predecessors, he found the facility to be "broken, filthy, and almost a total wreck from end to end." The visiting inspector concurred. The only real improvements in recent years had been conversion of the lighthouse lamps from lard oil to kerosene, the acquisition of a new casting for the fog siren, and construction of a hitching post for visiting horses.

It was not surprising that accomplishments would be small and the station would from time to time be allowed to fall into disrepair. Life was so arduous as to be overwhelming for the light keepers. In 1889, keeper Ryan wrote that the second assistant had gone crazy and had been taken by the first assistant and his brother to the constable in the nearby town of Olema. Then, rather mysteriously, three days later a new hand begins making entries in the station log book, and we are told that Ryan, too, had been "dismissed from the Lighthouse Service." A week later, a log entry notes that wind had blown rocks off the cliff, clogging the coal chute for 100 feet.

With events such as these, Point Reyes was by no means the most popular station in the early days of the Lighthouse Service. Thus, it was that keeper E. G. Chamberlin penned in the log:

Solitude, where are thy charms that sages have seen in thy face?
Better dwell in the midst of alarms than reign in this horrible place.

So city, friendship, and love
Divinely bestowed upon man,
O' had I the wings of a dove,
How I would taste you again. . . .

Another keeper, upon being reassigned to pleasant East Brother light, simply wrote in the log that he was "returning to the U.S.A."

After 1889 those hardy keepers who managed to withstand life at Point Reyes found they had new neighbors. With shipwrecks continuing, the Life-Saving Service had decided to make a second attempt at establishing a life-saving station in the area. The site selected was two and one-half miles north of the lighthouse on Point Reyes Beach. It is difficult to imagine a more dangerous location. Unlike calm Drake's Bay, the surf at Point Reyes Beach may well be the heaviest in California.

To face such conditions, the station was well-equipped and fully manned. There was a station house with quarters for the keeper and his family as well as for the crew of seven surfmen. There was a boathouse for the surfboat and the beach cart. Surfmen manned the pulling boat, maintained a lookout, and patrolled the beach for a mile on each side

Point Reyes Life-Saving Station on Point Reyes Beach. The larger building housed the keeper and crew; the smaller structure housed the surfboat, beach apparatus, and beach cart. Surfmen patrolled the beach for a mile in each direction. (San Francisco Maritime Museum)

The crew of the Point Reyes Life-Saving Station. Howard Underhill, soon to become the station's officer-in-charge, sits at center. 1923. (Howard Underhill)

The Life-Saving Service offered no accommodations for surfmen's families. As a result many stations were surrounded by shanties where underpaid surfmen and their families resided. Single men and the family of the keeper could live in the station itself. C. 1924. (Howard Underhill)

Auxiliary boathouse on Drake's Bay. Built about 1912, this structure allowed boat drills to be conducted in the calmer waters of Drake's Bay rather than on treacherous Point Reyes beach. Auxiliary boathouses provided surfmen with an additional boat which, at times, might be more convenient to a shipwreck than those at the main station. C. 1920's. (Howard Underhill)

of the station. Patrols were especially important at night and during thick weather when individuals or even entire wrecks might otherwise go undetected. The high winds were the worst aspect of the patrols, since the sand was blown with such force that it tore at the men's faces. Some wore goggles to protect their eyes. However, it was the surf that was the most dangerous. The crew had to practice boat drills in which they purposely capsized their surfboat and then righted it amidst the heavy breakers. The surfman's job was more dangerous than light keeping; among the eight-man crew, four would be lost during the first four years of the Point Reyes Life-Saving Station's existence.

In former years light keepers had spotted ships flying distress signals and were helpless to aid those on board. They had also seen ships ground on shore and were poorly equipped to help the seamen reach safety or to care for them once they were ashore. Now, with a new 12-inch steam fog whistle, all the keepers had to do was sound five or six short, sharp blasts followed by a blast of 15 seconds and the surfmen were alerted that a ship was in distress. Lyle gun, breeches buoy, surfboat, and two dozen more pieces of rescue equipment would then be rushed to the scene by the life-saving crew.

The incredible wind and fog at Point Reyes had not gone unnoticed by the Weather Bureau. By the turn of the century, the Weather Bureau had built a substantial station at the light facility. A large signal display station was built at the head of the stairs leading from the keepers' dwelling to the lighthouse. Storm warning flags were flown to alert mariners that foul weather was at hand. More modern means of communication were used as well: a telephone line linked the point with San Francisco and an underwater communications cable stretched from Point Reyes to the Farallon Islands.

Thus, the point was now watched over and protected by the Lighthouse Service, the Life-Saving Service and the Weather Bureau. The area was a challenge for all three.

The light station itself was growing, too. Two additional keepers' residences had been built as well as a barn, storehouses, coalhouse, and a lime house. The lime house had a pit measuring six by eight feet and four feet deep where lime was mixed to whitewash the station. On the cliffs along the stairs leading to the lighthouse several large water tanks had been built. Even the internal communication system was improved; the old call bell system of ringing for a keeper was replaced by six inter-communicating telephones, complete with a miniature switchboard and cranks.

The epicenter of the 1906 earthquake was nearby at Olema, but a station built to withstand those high winds was little bothered by the tremor that destroyed so many lesser structures. The lighthouse was undamaged, although the lens had some guides bent and the lamp stand

In 1928 the Coast Guard built its Point Reyes Lifeboat Station on Drake's Bay, subsequently abandoning its Point Reyes Beach facility. Nearest structure is the boathouse. In the distance the officer-in-charge's home and various outbuildings can be seen. 1977. (R. Shanks)

Graves of the surfmen lost in the breakers at Point Reyes Beach (R. Shanks)

inside was displaced. A chimney was knocked from one building and the cistern cracked. Otherwise, nothing was harmed.

The Point Reyes station had put its troublesome early years behind; and visitors, among them author Jack London and famed anthropologist T. T. Waterman, toured the spectacular and beautiful lighthouse. They were not disappointed as keepers opened the heavy iron door and showed them the gleaming lens sitting amidst a wood-paneled room. Often a wickie would release the brake, open a small, round hatch, and let the 180-pound weight begin its two-hour journey down the drop tube. The lens would cast beautiful, little rainbows on the walls as it revolved. Below the lantern room was the old lamp cleaning room where tools and oil were stored. Some old-timers still called it the "sleeping room," although attendants were not supposed to doze when they stood watch here.

The 1920's and 1930's saw further changes at the point. As early as 1912 the Life-Saving Service had built an auxiliary boathouse on Drake's Bay to provide a readily available surfboat for shipwrecks on the point's southeast side. This had proven to be a favorable location and boat drills soon came to be conducted in the calm bay waters. Then, in 1915, the Life-Saving Service was merged with the Revenue Cutter Service to become the modern Coast Guard. The Coast Guard continued the trend of converting the old life-saving stations (equipped originally with hand-launched pulling boats) into modern lifeboat stations. Lifeboat stations featured heavy, gasoline-powered, 36-foot motor lifeboats, which required a marine railway for launching. Point Reyes Beach was so rough that a marine railway would be washed away by the surf. It therefore became necessary to build a new station on Drake's Bay if power boats were to replace pulling boats. A fine site was selected near Chimney Rock. The new station included a handsome home for officer-in-charge Howard A. Underhill and his family, a large boathouse with crews' quarters, office, and galley, and—among a number of other structures—a lookout tower on the hill above the boathouse. Inside the boathouse was a 36-foot, class "H," motor lifeboat, the pride of the Coast Guardsmen.

Bolinas Bay had already gotten a new lifeboat station in 1915, after residents had watched helplessly when the steamer *Hanalei* struck Duxbury Reef and went down with a loss of 23 lives. A shocked public had demanded a new station and had gotten one. There was a well-built, no-nonsense station house and a double garage, along with a picturesque lookout tower that resembled a small lighthouse. The only real trouble with Bolinas Bay was that the harbor was so silted up that rescue craft could get across the bar only at high tide. For mariners unfortunate enough to meet disaster during low water, Coast Guardsmen were reduced to running along the bluffs offering help from the

Breeches buoy rescue on Point Reyes Beach, January, 1913. Surfmen bring a sailor ashore from steam schooner Samoa. *(San Francisco Maritime Museum)*

shore. This was not quite as big a disadvantage as it would seem, since a significant percentage of the station's calls were from vacationing swimmers and small boats only a short distance from shore.

But if low tides aggravated Coast Guard lifesavers, high winds continued to plague the light keepers. Back at the lighthouse, one veteran had been stranded for 36 hours in the tower by high winds. Any attempt to climb the stairs would have seen the old keeper blown off the stairway and over the cliff.

One night, assistant Perry Hunter had a more frightening experience. The wind was blowing so loudly that he found it impossible to sleep. Hunter rose from his bed and walked toward the kitchen, intending to make a pot of coffee. A moment later, a 2"x12" timber blew through the bedroom window, moving "like an arrow." The plank shot across the room, sweeping the bed and snagging Hunter's bedclothes as it moved. The plank slammed into the far wall, pinning the bedclothes to the wall. For years afterward, keeper Hunter shuddered at the thought of what would have happened had he remained in bed a few moments longer.

Point Reyes was one of those light stations where a man might wake up in the morning to find the masts of a sunken ship protruding from the water below the light. It was a hard station, much like Cape Mendocino and Punta Gorda, but by the early 1920's conditions were beginning to improve.

Education had come to Point Reyes, too. In 1921, a school was established on the Mendoza Ranch; and children of light keepers, Coast Guardsmen, and Weather Bureau employees mingled with the offspring of local ranchers. The first teacher even lived at the light station, sharing a house with the family of a meteorologist.

The road across the point had been improved, too, and the Lighthouse Service took advantage of this fact by shipping coal on the Northwestern Pacific Railroad and having it trucked to the station.

Such improvements in transportation and communication meant that the Weather Bureau's need for its Point Reyes facility lessened too; and in 1927 the weather station was turned over to the Lighthouse Service to be utilized as a keeper's dwelling. Two years later a powerhouse with generators and air compressors was built beside the lighthouse, and air replaced steam in the fog signals. The frame powerhouse was paneled inside to match the interior of the lighthouse. It contained an office, workshop, and storage room, in addition to a spacious engine room. Earlier, the fog signals had been converted to powerful air horns, run by Doak gas engines with their big wheels. The air horns had proven so powerful that they shook the cliffs, dislodging rock. Large areas had to be cemented over to prevent falling rock from bombarding the fog signal building. By 1934 the fog signals were removed from the lower terrace and placed in a new frame structure just a few feet below the lighthouse. This eliminated half of the 600-plus steps wickies had to climb at least twice daily.

Launching the surfboat during a boat drill on Drake's Bay. 1924. (Howard Underhill)

The new motor lifeboat had made things easier, too, eliminating hours of rowing in the old pulling boats. However, the new craft was no cure-all. In August, 1929, a pleasure boat was disabled, about to drift into the breakers at Point Reyes Beach. The "36" (as such motor lifeboats were called), managed to get a line on her, only to have the rope foul the rescue craft's propeller. Then the "36" and her crew were summarily swept into the surf themselves, the motor lifeboat being tossed up high on the beach by the breakers.

About this time the indefatigable Fred Kreth was keeper at the light. A fishing boat with a crew of three hit the rocks at the point. The boat was a total loss, but the fishermen managed to find refuge on a beach. They were ashore all right, but found themselves trapped by cliffs. The Coast Guard received the call, rushing to the beach in the "36." Once there, Captain Underhill and his men found that the surf was too high for a sea rescue. They returned to the lifeboat station and drove back to the point. Then they rigged lines and dropped them down to the beach. There was no response to their calls, so a Coast Guardsman climbed 75 feet straight down the cliff. Once at the beach, he found it deserted. The fishermen were found safe, receiving aid at the lighthouse from keeper Kreth. Alone, Kreth had descended the cliff and rescued the crew, singlehandedly pulling three men to safety.

In 1930 Gustav Zetterquist came to the lighthouse as an assistant keeper. Born in Sweden, he had begun his career as a surfman, serving at Jackson Park Station on Lake Michigan. His wife eventually became postmistress of the tiny post office in the lighthouse dwelling. Together they would raise a fine family at the point. They would also see many changes.

An electric power line was completed to Bolinas in the late 1930's. In the lighthouse, the oil-vapor mantle was removed from the lamp, wiring installed, and a 1,500-watt bulb mounted in its place. The wickies liked the new system since it eliminated a tedious lighting-up process, and no longer required that adjustments be made during the night. More importantly, the bulb was brighter and absolutely clean. With the oil-vapor mantle gone, smoke and carbon were eliminated, making the lens far easier to keep clean. Oil handling was virtually eliminated. The old clockwork system was maintained intact and a kerosene lantern kept on standby duty should both the commercial power and the emergency generators fail. They did. As late as the 1970's, once or twice a year Coast Guardsmen would have to light the oil lantern and set the weight in motion. About 1972, officer-in-charge Gerald "Andy" Anderson even had to buy a new kerosene lantern, since he found himself using the antique system surprisingly often. It was probably the last oil lantern ever purchased for a California lighthouse.

Early pulling lifeboats were, of course, unpowered and depended upon the endurance of their crews for their range and speed. Arena Cove Life-Saving Station. 1904. (Robert J. Lee)

By 1908, 36-foot, Class "E," power lifeboats had come to Humboldt Bay and Fort Point station in San Francisco. Notice that the rear air compartment has been expanded from that of the old pulling lifeboats and the engine placed in the boat's stern. 1927. (Harry Hoffman)

By the late 1920's, newer Class "H," 36-foot motor lifeboats were beginning to replace the old Class "E" boats. The engine was placed amidship and the end compartments shortened. This was Point Reyes' first power lifeboat, shown here after fouling her propeller in a tow line and stranding on Point Reyes Beach. 1929. (Howard Underhill)

Last of the old wooden, 36-foot motor lifeboats was Number 36542. She served at Arena Cove, Point Reyes, Bodega Bay, and Fort Point. Shown here on Bodega Bay in 1975, this is the boat which mysteriously ran ashore on Point Reyes beach with her crew missing. Repaired, she is still in service today. (R. Shanks)

While the light station retained much of its timeless character, there were vast changes elsewhere. The advent of World War II caused the Army to place soldiers at the strategic point and improvised barracks were set up at the light station. The lighthouse was far from lonely now; and along with the post office there was even a post exchange.

With the end of the war, the soldiers left. Now the cliffs were watched over largely by the Zetterquist children. There was fishing from the rocks and occasional school parties, but son Charley seems to remember the coal chute best. He recalls his father tossing a couple of buckets of water on the chute to lubricate it so that lumber could be slid down to the lighthouse. The water worked more than adequately and the boards went flashing down the chute with such speed that they became airborne, and aided by the wind, sailed away to sea. One of Charley's young friends decided to ride the chute and greased the bottom of a box for added speed. He, too, got better results than he bargained for. He rocketed off down the chute, only managing to stop himself after his never-to-be-forgotten ride had carried him almost to the powerhouse wall.

The Zetterquists loved their life at the point and served the station for 21 years, until 1951. From then until automation in 1975, the station was staffed by Coast Guardsmen. The powerhouse next to the lighthouse was slightly renovated to include radio-beacon equipment, a watch room with weather station, generators, air compressors, storage batteries, and an air tank for the fog signal. The versatile building also still served as a workshop and storage room. The light, fog signal, and radio beacon were conveniently located near each other and all three could be monitored by one man. It was a far cry from the early days when watches were rotated with one man on duty at the old lower fog signal, another at the light, and a third working above at the dwellings.

In 1960, the lovely, old, two-story dwelling was razed and a modern, four-plex apartment building erected in its place. A new office and garage were also built.

This same year there was a strange and disturbing tragedy involving the life-saving station's 36-foot motor lifeboat. This was not the original "36," but one built at Curtis Bay, Maryland, in 1953. On the cold, rainy night of November 23, 1960, the "36" was returning to Drake's Bay after towing a disabled fishing boat into Bodega Bay. About three miles north of the lighthouse, the two-man crew radioed the lifeboat station to expect them to tie up in about an hour. Then nothing else was ever heard. The Coast Guardsmen at the station became concerned, and huge waves along the coast did not ease their fears. But the motor lifeboat, number 36542, had been built of the finest wood to withstand the worst conditions the sea could offer, and for decades such craft had been the standard rescue boats on the North Coast. She was self-bailing and self-righting, and had sealable compartments so that she could even withstand a hole in the side. For all practical purposes, she was unsinkable. Why hadn't she come home?

The next morning, Thanksgiving Day, the "36" was found. She had run ashore on Point Reyes Beach between the RCA Communications Station and the lighthouse. Her motor was still running and her propeller turning. She was in sound condition, completely seaworthy, but her crew had disappeared.

A massive search began, using Coast Guard patrol boats, planes, and helicopters. Coast Guardsmen and volunteers hiked through miles of soft sand, and mounted posses covered both the Marin and Sonoma coastlines. It was to no avail; by the end of the year two bodies washed ashore and were identified as those of the missing crewmen.

What had happened? How could two highly skilled seamen be lost while aboard a perfectly seaworthy boat? The "36" required only minor repairs and was back in service by February, 1961. She is still in service today, the last active "36" in the United States, operating out of Bodega Bay and San Francisco Bay since 1968 when the Point Reyes Lifeboat Station was closed. Her current crew think they know what happened. In the dark night, a large, freak wave could have hit the vessel by surprise, capsizing the boat and spilling the crew into the sea. The "36," responding as she had been built to do, righted herself and kept on going, moving swiftly out of reach of the Coast Guardsmen in the water. With their boat gone, the cold, rough seas and strong currents would make reaching safety impossible. It was one of the point's saddest maritime tragedies.

There were few changes through the 1960's and into the 1970's. The faithful beacon continued to flash once every five seconds from its lofty perch. In thick weather, every twenty-seven seconds the big diaphragm air horns would blast away for three seconds. Point Reyes lighthouse was probably the best preserved and most traditionally operated light on the entire coast, rivaled only by Point Arena.

The last officer-in-charge at Point Reyes, Tom Smith, could operate the light just as had his predecessors a century before. During power failures, he had to light the oil lantern, insert the old crank, and wind the weight in the same manner and using the same equipment as principal keeper John C. Bull had used. When automation approached, things were little changed. Smith still found it occasionally necessary to wrap his arms tightly around the railing of the stairway leading down to the light, lest the wind carry him away like a piece of Gustav Zetterquist's lumber.

Automation meant removing the fog signal building and replacing it with a cement structure containing a new reflecting light, electric fog signal, and the radio-beacon equipment. Contractors found the work so difficult that there were several years of delay before the structure was completed. The chute was now gone, but a combination stairway and cart track replaced it and materials again had to be lowered using a flatcar and winch. The work finally finished, the station was unmanned and converted to automatic operation in June, 1975. The Point Reyes National Seashore assumed control over the facility, and park rangers moved into the dwelling as keepers moved out.

Today the National Park Service has reopened the lighthouse to the public. Visitors are able to tour daily, weather permitting.

The lifeboat stations still stand as well. The Point Reyes Lifeboat Station on Drake's Beach is owned by the Park Service. It was closed in 1968, having been largely superseded by a modern Coast Guard lifeboat station opened at Bodega Bay on July 6, 1963. Most rescue calls now entailed towing commercial fishing boats into Bodega Harbor rather than rescuing steamers stranded at the point. The station at Bolinas Bay is now used as College of Marin's Biology Station, since the Coast Guard closed it in 1946. Up on the Bolinas Highlands, the picturesque lookout tower remains, too, now used as a private residence. All of the old Coast Guard buildings remain in their original condition and deserve preservation as important links in our maritime heritage.

A shallow bay entrance necessitated assigning smaller, lightweight surfboats for rescue work at Bolinas Bay. C. 1940. (U S. Coast Guard)

Bolinas Bay Coast Guard Station was built in 1915 to watch over Duxbury Reef and nearby beaches. Stairway in background leads up to lookout tower. C. 1940. (U.S. Coast Guard)

Bolinas Bay station's lookout tower. Traditionally, lookouts literally stood since the Life-Saving Service held that a man standing was more alert than one sitting. C. 1940. (U.S. Coast Guard)

FARALLON ISLANDS

The Farallon Islands are well named. *Los Farallones* is the old Spanish mariner's term for small, pointed sea islands; and the Farallons indeed rise like stone icebergs 23 miles westward of the San Francisco Bay entrance. The rocky, barren islets are scattered in a rough, broken line over seven miles long.

Remarked upon by nearly all of the early coastal explorers, the Farallons were to provide an incredible bounty to those determined to exploit it. On July 24, 1579, Sir Francis Drake used the islands to replenish his larder, drawing upon the "great store of seals and birds." It was the Russians, however, who first extensively utilized the resources of the Farallons. Arriving about 1810, three seasons of effort yielded 200,000 fur seals. Later, to supply Fort Ross with salted sea lion meat, a base was established on the islands during 1819-1820. The Russian and Aleut crew lived in huts covered with sea lion skins and burned animal fat for fuel. When scurvy broke out and the men became too weak to hunt, it was the islands' murre and gull eggs that kept the miserable party alive.

By the 1840's the Russians had left California, and for a number of years after the Farallons were viewed as no more than hazards to navigation. Famed clipper ships were frequently fogbound for days as they sought San Francisco Bay, and the unmarked islands represented a terrible menace. With the Gold Rush, the Farallons gained new prominence. Thousands of gold seekers had risked their lives sailing past the islands; and this, in itself, makes them noteworthy.

The newcomers soon hungered for more than gold. Safely in San Francisco, they realized they had to eat. One of their mainstays, chicken eggs, were rare and expensive in the California of 1850. Anyone who could supply fresh eggs was in a position to make a fortune. Egg-gathering companies were formed, and bands of determined men set sail for the Farallons. They wore baggy shirts with huge pockets and carried guns. The capacious "egg shirts" were for stashing murre and gull eggs while climbing about the islands raiding nests. The guns were for keeping competing egg companies at a distance. Collecting soon was being carried on at a furious pace. Millions upon millions of eggs were shipped to San Francisco. One boatload alone left with one thousand dozen eggs on board. In what were to become known as the Farallon Egg

Farallon Islands lighthouse was the farthest offshore of all California's lighthouses. C. 1865. (Bancroft Library)

Wars, hunting bird eggs began to mirror hunting gold. Ugly brawls and "shoot-out" incidents occurred.

The Lighthouse Board's construction program on the California coast was instituted at this time, and in 1852 the largest of the islands, 317-foot-high Southeast Farallon, was chosen as the site of the West Coast's third lighthouse. The contractors dispatched the bark *Oriole* with a construction crew and materials. When they arrived, armed egg pickers refused to allow the crew to land. The egg men were not about to allow any lighthouse on the Farallons. Its flashing light might well frighten the birds away and, with them, a highly profitable business. Never mind a few shipwrecks, they reasoned. The workmen, paid to build lighthouses, not to fight pitched battles, returned to San Francisco to report that construction had been stymied.

The local lighthouse authorities were appalled at these events. A Coast Survey steamer, crewed by well-armed United States seamen, was sent out to recapture the Farallons. The professional fighting men drew a different response than had the unarmed construction workers. The

Southeast Farallon, shown here, is the largest in the island chain. The lighthouse is atop the highest peak. 1969. (U.S. Coast Guard)

First dwelling was this little stone house. Later, after larger quarters were provided, school was held here for a time. C. 1920. (U.S. Coast Guard)

egg gatherers quickly re-evaluated their stance and decided that a lighthouse would be a welcome addition after all.

Engineers chose the very summit of Southeast Farallon as the light tower site. So steep was the rocky peak that residences and other buildings would have to be located on the plain below. Both a dangerous landing and brittle, crumbling cliffs hindered construction. The plain, fortunately, was ample, and workers were able to establish a construction camp on the island. The workmen began the exhausting chore of carrying all materials by hand up the 300-foot peak. Bricks, for example, could only be carried four or five at a time; and the pace became so grueling that a desperate sit-down strike was staged. The major demand was for a mule; and shortly thereafter one was provided, although it arrived in a terribly seasick condition.

The mule soon recovered and work progressed rapidly. Stone was quarried on the island and then used to form the shell of the tower. A brick lining was added to the shell. The completed beacon soon stood proud, although dark. The lens had not arrived from France as scheduled. Probably to the relief of the egg gatherers, the lighthouse crew then sailed off on the *Oriole* to build another lighthouse, leaving the Farallons unlighted. It was the fall of 1853.

This masonry chimney is all that remains of the original blow-hole fog signal. The chimney still works as the blowing hair and slacks of this Coast Guardsman's wife indicate. C. 1950. (San Francisco Public Library)

On December 12, 1854, the French ship *St. Joseph* arrived in San Francisco loaded with wine and a first order lens. The wine was for San Francisco and the lens for the Farallons. A crew was dispatched to the island, and with utmost care, the men safely landed the lens and carried it up the peak. Its installation would signal the end of the exhausting Farallons project and a quick return to the pleasures of San Francisco. Then, to everyone's consternation, difficulties began to be experienced. The huge brass and glass jewel did not seem to fit the tower. Doubt began to set in. Doubt was soon followed by the realization that a terrible engineering error had been made. The tower was too small for the lens.

The stunned crew had only one option. They tore down the tower and built a larger lighthouse. The final result was a handsome, white, masonry tower topped with a lantern room painted black. The structure stood 41 feet high and featured two galleries. It was first lighted on January 1, 1856.

Two years later, lighthouse engineer Hartmann Bache decided, quite correctly, that the Farallons needed a fog signal as well. Finding a natural cave which formed a blowhole, he reasoned that air forced through the opening by wave action could be channeled up through a brick chimney to a whistle. Thus, with each rush of a wave, the displaced air would blow the fog signal.

In normal seas, the device worked exceptionally well. During storms it blared unceasingly. But during calm weather, when seas were still, the whistle was mute. Unfortunately, fog often accompanies calm seas on the California coast. Often, when the whistle was most needed, there was insufficient wave action to activate it. Still, it was better than nothing, and the blowhole whistle remained in use until a fierce storm destroyed it in 1871. It was replaced by a conventional steam siren.

The fears of the egg gatherers were unfulfilled; and despite the light and fog whistle, the birds remained on the island. Fierce competition continued among the hunters and seemed to increase as they depleted the bird population. A single group, the Farallon Egg Company, had acquired exclusive gathering rights from the government in 1856, but poachers were common and violence flared periodically. Hundreds of

More reliable than the blow-hole whistle, after 1871 these huge steam-powered sirens were the fog signals which warned ships away from the Farallons. (U.S. Coast Guard)

These two duplexes were built far below the lighthouse, probably about 1875. They served as quarters for light keepers for nearly a century. (U.S. Coast Guard)

thousands of eggs continued to be shipped to San Francisco with some of the light keepers even joining the hunt to earn extra money. The keepers also supplemented their meager income by hunting seals, whose powdered whiskers, according to one source, were popular with the city's Chinese as a sure cure for impotence.

The exploitation of the bird and animal life continued during the first two decades of the light station's existence. The Egg Wars were the source of sporadic and increasing violence. The unruly egg men became so annoying that the keepers complained to the Lighthouse Service. Annoyance turned to danger when, in 1881, a rival group decided to break the monopoly of the Farallon Egg Company. Three boats of armed men came out from San Francisco and stormed Southeast Farallon. The attack had been anticipated and the defenders were behind a wall of gunny sacks, guns at the ready. Rifles and pistols blazed away and an invader was killed. Finally, with four casualties, the defenders surrendered. Things were by now so out of hand that a U.S. Marshal and a platoon of soldiers sailed out to eject the egg gatherers and raze their huts. Later, however, egg collecting was resumed and continued at a high level until about 1890 when sales declined.

For some time the egg business had been only an unsavory sidelight to the principal island occupation of light keeping. The declining market, combined with the Lighthouse Service's opposition to the practice, served to discourage "egg picking." When first assistant Louis Engelbrecht fell while gathering eggs and broke both legs, it was just about the end of the egg business. No one was henceforth allowed to land on the Farallons without approval of the District Superintendent of Lighthouses in San Francisco. Commercial destruction of bird and animal life was, from then on, limited to an occasional sealing boat that would come by and "snatch a couple of seals."

In 1909, through the efforts of conservationists, most of the Farallons were designated a bird sanctuary and the pillaging came to an end. From that time on, the keepers worked diligently to protect bird and animal life and must be given credit for making the sanctuary a success.

The years from the 1880's until about 1906 saw the islands largely come under the care of two highly dedicated light-keeping families, the O'Caines and the Beemans. They represented the finest traditions of the profession, and they would be the last families to endure the total isolation of the earliest days on the islands.

When William Beeman and Cyrus O'Caine brought their wives and children to the Farallons, it was as though moving to another world. The tender *Madroño* served the entire California coast alone, and she could only call at the islands four times a year. There was no other communication with the mainland. The families did well with what they had. They had landed safely and found the frame houses to be cozy and well built. There were so many children that school would be held in the original stone dwelling, although the keepers soon found that live-in teachers resigned every time the *Madroño* returned. Wild Belgian hares, introduced years earlier, had multiplied spectacularly; and rabbit stew, fresh fish, and eggs provided many a meal. Abalone could be gathered and kept alive in a small hole filled by sea spray. Turkeys, chickens, and goats were raised, supplying fresh meat. While bird droppings often fouled the water in the cistern, the guano had created a rich site for gardening. Vegetables and flowers grew well, although the rabbits made growing carrots none too easy. Sometimes the Italian fishermen from San Francisco, grateful for the lighthouse's presence, would come by and toss ashore presents of red wine and fresh crab.

The *Madroño*'s arrival on "boat day" was a major event. All the necessities of civilization had to be landed, including hay and grain for a horse named Jenny and a mule called Patty. Both animals pulled the little flatcar on the railroad that ran from the landing up to the dwellings and down to the fog signal. It was a real horse- (or, more usually, mule-) car line with switches, trestles, and 3,559 feet of track that leaped gulleys and ravines to provide an important means of moving all the supplies that landed each quarter. This included tons of coal for the first-class steam siren, which blasted once every 45 seconds for five painful seconds. Patty, the mule, had to pull most of that coal; and when she heard the *Madroño*'s whistle, she knew work was about to begin. Patty would then take off, and the keepers would have to run about the island trying to catch her.

The keepers worked hard, too. It was a steep, 300-foot-high climb from the residences up to the lighthouse. There were no railings in those days; and rain, wind, and lightning made the trek difficult and dangerous. Watches had to be stood each night: all night at the beacon, and in thick weather down at the fog signal building on the flats, too. Once the lens' clockwork drive failed, and the keepers spent the entire night rotating the lens by hand so that it would show its characteristic white flash once every minute.

Whatever its shortcomings, the children seemed to have loved their island life. There were countless, fascinating places to play and a multitude of animals and birds. Each Christmas season would see the *Madroño* arrive with presents and even a Christmas tree. Then the children had to stay away from the landing while presents were brought ashore. When the great day arrived, keeper Beeman played Santa Claus.

Despite the happy times, the Farallons had one devastating and terrible drawback. There was no communication with the mainland, save for the rare visits by the tender. Any communication must await her return. During times of sickness, this could be too long.

"Boat Day" on the Farallons was always exciting. A boatload of supplies is being worked in under the derrick at old North Landing. The tender Sequoia *waits offshore. C. 1920's. (U.S. Coast Guard)*

One night Southeast Farallon glowed as bonfires burned all around the island. Diphtheria had broken out and the children were gravely ill. Frantic parents fed the fires all through the night in hopes that a passing ship might see their distress signal. Finally, a sailing ship noticed the fires and reported the news in San Francisco. The following morning the *Madroño* steamed out, a doctor on board. The rapid trip from San Francisco had left the poor doctor quite seasick, but he was well enough to perceive that action must be taken immediately. He ministered to the critically ill children and then ordered mattresses, blankets, and the like burned. However, the delay had been too long. Two O'Caine children died.

Tragedy struck the Beeman family as well. In December, 1898, the Beeman's young son, Royal, eleven years old, became desperately ill. The only boat on the island was a 14-foot Whitehall, used on calm days for fishing just off shore. On this day, a winter storm had come in and the sea was breaking heavily. The parents decided that an attempt must be made to reach San Francisco in the rowboat, a trip of well over twenty miles.

First assistant Engelbrecht volunteered to accompany the Beemans. The boat was made ready. Because of the tremendous seas, Royal, his mother, and his two-month-old sister—too young to leave behind—, were all placed, warmly wrapped, in the bottom of the boat. Launching a boat at the Farallons is always hazardous, under these conditions especially so; but Beeman and Engelbrecht succeeded in safely getting under way. They hoped to row all the way to San Francisco.

It was to be a terrible trip, with breaking seas, heavy winter rain, and—at times—hail. There was but one refuge between the Farallons and the mainland, the *San Francisco Lightship*, anchored just off the bar. Three hours later the rowboat reached the light vessel.

The lightship was unable to assist those in the little boat. She could not leave her station to take them ashore and was too small to have a doctor on board. Ironically, it would be less than a year before the San Francisco light vessel would be equipped with a wireless and would become the nation's first lightship to broadcast a ship-to-shore radio message. However, in late 1898 she was still without a radio.

Mail call brought families down to the landing hoping for news from the mainland. Principal keeper John Kunder distributes envelopes. 1929. (U.S. Coast Guard)

Thus Beeman and Engelbrecht continued rowing (and using a small sail they had rigged) toward the dangerous San Francisco bar. As they were about to attempt what probably would have been a fatal crossing, the pilot boat *America* saw them. The *America* came alongside and took all safely on board, even hoisting the rowboat on deck. The pilot boat then came about and raced toward San Francisco.

Reaching San Francisco, Royal was rushed to a hospital. A team of doctors tried to save the youngster's life, but it was, again, too late. The child died.

The O'Caines were to lose three children on the Farallons (two to diphtheria and one who fell off the landing and drowned while the *Madroño* was calling). Royal's death meant the loss of four children from the islands in a relatively short period. The tragedy would be a major factor in the Beemans' decision to leave the Farallons, transferring to mainland lighthouses at Point Arguello and, later, Point Loma. The O'Caines and their three surviving children remained on the Farallons.

After these tragedies the Lighthouse Service took steps to improve communication and transportation to the Farallons. Not only did the lightship receive a wireless in 1899, but that same year the gasoline schooner *Ida A.* was contracted to call once every two weeks at both the Farallons and the lightship, bringing mail and supplies.

At about this same time, an amazing 18-mile-long, undersea cable was laid from Point Reyes to the Farallon Islands. It allowed direct, instant communication between the islands and the mainland, except during storms when there was so much noise in the line that it was rendered useless. In 1903 the cable broke, and the Point Reyes lifesaving crew was called to grapple for the cable. The surfmen were successful both in recovering the cable and in buoying it. Then they assisted the crew of the steamer *Alexander Volta* in splicing the cable, thus restoring communication.

All these modern conveniences did not mean that the Farallons station was becoming an ordinary place to live. The multitude of birds alone set the place apart. At least one species of night bird would hurl itself at any sudden light. This made lighting a match at night a bit hazardous. Perhaps a few surprised wickies were cured of smoking. Bird droppings were always a problem too. During the long, hot days of late summer, after several months without rain, the tops of the rocks would whiten like snow as guano accumulated. The stench could be quite foul; even passing ships could smell the islands. The birds also made washing a chore. Droppings fouled laundry that was hung out to dry.

The Lighthouse Service had spent a great deal of effort building the cistern and catch basin about 1880. The rocky island resisted cutting, and the engineers resorted to blasting the rock away. This revealed several veins of orangish, mineralized water unfit for drinking. When cement work began, the water kept the mortar from drying, and all of the brickwork had to be removed. Eventually, the problem was solved by cutting a hole through solid rock in the cistern bottom, all the way to a bluff below. The water thus continually ran out the hole, allowing the mortar to dry. Once the cistern was completed, the birds freely used the catchment area, fouling the drinking water (something that the Russian sealers had found to their sorrow decades earlier). Despite an impressive 40,000-gallon capacity, the cistern would occasionally run dry, and fresh water would have to be brought from shore to supply the steam fog siren as well as for home use.

The keepers' dwellings included the original, one-and-a-half-story stone residence, which served as schoolhouse for a while and was then reconverted to a dwelling after the school was closed in 1900. A pair of two-story, frame dwellings, handsome, New England-style structures, had been added and came to serve as the principal residences for the keepers. In addition, there was a blacksmith shop, storage tanks, and other outbuildings. In 1905 the Navy established a wireless telegraph station on Southeast Farallon, and the wickies had new neighbors. Communication between buildings was improved by use of call bells, although a well-placed bolt of lightning once put the system out of commission temporarily.

Unquestionably, the most exciting thing about the Farallons was arriving or leaving. There was no wharf; the island's shore was too steep, rocky, and wave-washed to allow docking a boat except under exceptionally calm conditions. Landing usually required the dangerous maneuver of working a small boat in among the rocks and then transferring from boat to shore by means of an aerial ride at the end of a derrick.

There were two landings, old North Landing and South Landing. The choice of which landing to use depended upon sea conditions. If seas were rough at both landings, no one would be put ashore from the tender. North Landing was originally the preferred one; but by 1896 there had been so many narrow escapes that the derrick was removed to South Landing, and that locale was used more often.

The standard, early-day landing procedure was for the tender to put over a small boat some distance off the island. On calm days at North Landing the boat could be worked in close to some steps there. On rougher days South Landing's derrick could be used. A wide range of contrivances were used—some still in use today—to swing people up from the boat onto the island. Simplest was a board, about five feet square, with ropes running up from each corner. Those going ashore were rowed beneath the derrick's boom, the board was lowered, a passenger or two clambered on, and then they were hoisted up twenty or thirty feet and swung ashore. It was quite a ride, and not infre-

With the Magnolia's arrival, the old Lighthouse Service derrick will once again swing cargo bags and relief keepers up onto the island. The derrick is still in use today at South Landing. (U.S. Coast Guard)

Coming ashore at Farallon Islands light was never easy, although this woman managed it sitting in an armchair. C. 1930's. (San Francisco Public Library)

"The basket" was a common landing technique: an aerial ride never to be forgotten. 1952. (U.S. Coast Guard)

quently, newcomers would refuse to ride it. It could be dangerous; the rider could be washed off by unexpected swells, or the rider could lose his grip and fall into the sea. In 1905 the derrick itself collapsed. The principal skill in riding the thing was to hang on tight and distribute the passenger's weight so that it did not start spinning.

There were some innovative substitutes for the board. For a time a sturdy, wooden ship's chair was tied to the hook, and one could come ashore sitting, albeit none too comfortably. Later, a box-like affair proved popular, especially since it had sides to help prevent riders from falling out. A canvas "basket" had the same merits and eventually became a Coast Guard favorite. Riders often stood in the basket as they came ashore. The basket was followed by the "Billy Pugh net," a circular cage of ropes with a platform for standing. The Billy Pugh net has great flexibility and is purported to be unsinkable. It still is a preferred method of transferring personnel directly from the deck of 82-foot Coast Guard patrol boats to the island, eliminating the necessity of putting a small boat over the side. A final, classic technique—again, still in use—is to put a small boat over the side of a tender and work it in under the derrick. A line runs from the boat's bow to its stern. The derrick hook is lowered and fitted through an O-shaped center section in the boat's line. The entire boat, occupants and all, is then hoisted ashore.

Regardless of which method was used, all had their shortcomings. Small boats might be pitch-poled, capsized, or swamped. Occupants could be swept off baskets, board, nets, and chairs as unexpected swells appeared. When lifting small boats from the water, these same swells can rush up from underneath and dump those aboard into the sea. Even modern patrol boats find that it requires real seamanship to avoid being washed sideways onto hidden rocks. Patrol boats can also accidentally knock riders off a Billy Pugh net if the boat rises at the wrong moment.

Over the years, some things, like the landing, never changed. Earthquakes were that way. There had been many during the years of the O'Caines and the Beemans, but none like the one that destroyed San Francisco in 1906. The Great Quake apparently did little damage to the islands, at least the Lighthouse Service Annual Reports fail to mention anything of note. However, a most curious happening was reported off

Hoisting a small boat was still another mode of reaching the island. Coast Guard buoy tender Magnolia *stands by in the distance, pumping water and fuel ashore. 1949. (U.S. Coast Guard)*

the islands. The steamer *Mongolia* reported that the 1906 earthquake caused a "mountain of rock" to be lifted from the sea about 15 miles southwest of the Farallons. The incident was said to have occurred in eleven fathoms of water. Although the "mountain" was never again reported, the U.S. Geodetic and Topographic Survey department considered it a reliable sighting.

The advent of World War I caused the complement of the Navy station to be temporarily boosted to nine men. Although this would again be reduced to four or five personnel after the war, light keepers would continue to have Navy families as neighbors for several decades. There was also reportedly a Weather Station on the islands for a time during the early years of the twentieth century.

The 1920's included some of the most notable of the island's light keepers: Kunder, Cobb, Johnson, Atkinson, and others. Many were among the most distinguished in the Lighthouse Service.

George D. Cobb, for example, served in the Lighthouse Service for 40 years. Earlier in his career, he had been at Point Bonita light, south of Point Reyes. The day after Christmas in 1896 was cold at Point Bonita, with rain squalls and a gale wind. Suddenly, he saw a sailboat capsize and its three occupants go into the water. Cobb rushed to lower the lighthouse boat from its davits, no easy task, since it was exposed to the full fury of the wind. He succeeded in launching the boat, then rowed out past offshore rocks—hard work since the boat was designed to be handled by no less than two oarsmen. Despite the heavy seas and gale winds, Cobb reached the sailboat and pulled two unconscious men on board. Then he went after the third, who had drifted close to shore. The surf had battered its victim against the rocks, and he was unconscious and bleeding. Cobb worked the boat in among the rocks and pulled him aboard too. All three men recovered. For his efforts, Cobb received national recognition when he was awarded the Life-Saving Service's silver medal.

Cobb and his wife Theadora had since come to the Farallons. They were an experienced and highly respected light-keeping family and provided outstanding leadership while in charge at the Farallons. The younger keepers often called Theadora "Mother Cobb."

Then there was John Kunder. Kunder had been at Fort Point light in San Francisco when the 1906 earthquake destroyed the city. He was on watch in the tower at the moment the quake hit. Despite the violent shaking of the tower, Kunder refused to leave his post and kept Fort Point's beacon burning during and after the tremor. Kunder was a bachelor and a traditionalist. He still owned three "lens aprons," full-length robes once worn to prevent lint and dirt from touching the lens while early-day keepers worked in the lantern room. Choosing to live alone in Farallons' original stone dwelling, he rose to head keeper and loved the isolated life on the islands. He had had shore stations before, but John Kunder was an islander at heart. He seldom went ashore, even for his leave. He provided a calming effect when hotter tempers flared.

There were the newlyweds, J. Milford and Louise Johnson. They arrived in 1926 on their first assignment. Milford Johnson had been a motorman on San Francisco's streetcars, and Louise Johnson was a nurse. Shortly after their marriage, Milford joined the Lighthouse Service, a career destined to be far more exciting than operating trolleys. Louise's medical background would be highly valued on an isolated island with no doctor.

There were five Navy radiomen on the island as well as the five light keepers, and most of them had brought their wives and preschool children. Navy tugs alternated with the Lighthouse Service tenders in visiting the island so that the Farallons continued to receive mail and supplies once every two weeks—weather permitting. If the weather was too rough to allow a landing, then light-keeping families on shore leave had to find a hotel room in San Francisco and await better sea conditions. Sometimes tenders would journey all the way to the islands only to

J. Milford and Louise Johnson and their daughter Lexie, one of the Farallons'
distinguished light-keeping families. C. 1927. (Louise Johnson)

have the sea kick up, forcing the ship to return to port without un-
loading. Despite radios, the Farallons were still basically lonely and
inaccessible.

Landing could still be terrifying. In December, 1927, a Navy tug
brought out supplies and presents for Christmas. The keepers sent a
radio message warning of rough seas, but the landing was attempted
anyway. The tug put a small boat over, loaded with Christmas items.
The sea was so rough that as the boat approached the landing, it was
tossed violently about and a crewman was thrown from the boat. Along
with the sailor went most of the Christmas things. Both the supplies
and the Navy man were saved. Although the sailor soon was none the
worse for his dunking, the Christmas packages were badly damaged.

While the Navy used tugs, the Lighthouse Service had two fine
tenders. The *Sequoia* and the *Lupine* had replaced the aging *Madroño*
by now, and they did the Service's rough work, servicing the coastal
light stations. The little *Columbine* generally cared for stations and
buoys on the calmer waters of San Francisco Bay and the Sacramento-
San Joaquin Delta.

When the *Sequoia* or *Lupine* arrived at Farallons, a large pulling
boat was lowered away. Supplies would be stowed amidship in the
pulling boat and people placed only at each end. When the boat came
under the derrick, a cargo net would swing the supplies ashore. The net
was often quite full of heavy crates, and it was proper practice to pull
the net away from the boat as soon as it cleared the sides. Thus, if any
supplies fell from the net, they would not hit the boat. Once a netload
of heavy cans of provisions was being unloaded. Instead of swinging the
net away from the boat, the operator jerked it straight up, thirty feet
into the air. The stunned boat's occupants looked up, only to see the
derrick operator again jerk the boom, this time shoreward. A heavy case
of cans toppled out and fell thirty feet, hitting the center of the pulling
boat. Miraculously, the cans did not go through either passenger or
boat. All the passengers were still at the ends of the boat and were
missed.

Part of the problem in landing at the Farallons was that Navy
skippers sometimes were unfamiliar with the islands and under-
estimated the grave risks in landing personnel. When Milford and Louise
Johnson brought their three-week-old daughter Lexie back to the station from San Francisco, they encountered heavy seas. They were on
board the Navy tug *Undaunted* and, despite the Johnsons' protests, the
captain insisted on attempting to land them. The family was put over in

*During the nightly watches, keepers had to rewind the weight which powered the
lighthouse lens' clockwork drive. Veteran John Kunder drew this watch. C. 1929.
(U.S. Coast Guard)*

a small boat with two oarsmen and a coxswain. From the first the oarsmen had difficulty making headway. Soon it was obvious to all in the boat that there was no chance of a landing. Meanwhile, the *Undaunted* had drifted from view, so the oarsmen continued to fight toward the island. After a while the tug steamed back, and her master realized the hopelessness of the situation. The *Undaunted* blew her whistle, ordering the boat to return to the ship. In coming about, the small boat was almost tossed end for end by the waves. When the boat finally drew near the tug, conditions were so bad that the larger tug almost rammed the little craft. Finally, safely on board the tug, it was back to San Francisco for the Johnsons. The landing would be tried again when sea conditions improved.

While many landings were accomplished without much more trouble than a sea washing over a cargo net and soaking supplies, reaching the island continued to be difficult.

Medical attention, even with a radio and with Louise Johnson's nursing background, continued to be too distant and too long in coming. Thomas Atkinson had brought his wife to the Farallons after transferring from St. George Reef. During the Atkinsons' tenure, they became expectant parents. To everyone's surprise, the baby arrived eight weeks early. Radio messages were sent out requesting a doctor, but the child arrived before the physician. Louise Johnson took charge, and on February 19, 1927, little Delpha Atkinson was born. Under Mrs. Johnson's care both mother and child were doing well when the doctor arrived, quite seasick, on the tender. Seeing that all was well, the good physician charged the Atkinsons $50 for his trouble and spent the remainder of the day fishing.

Delpha Atkinson enjoys the distinction of being the only child born on the Farallon Islands in the twentieth century. Her only known predecessor was Farallone O'Caine, a daughter born to Mrs. Cyrus O'Caine, probably during the 1890's.

Delayed medical care did not always work out so well. Little Lexie Johnson became seriously ill. The child had five convulsions in one day and a desperate message was sent out by Navy radio, asking that any ship passing the Farallon Islands with a doctor on board stop and aid the youngster. The transport *Chaumont* soon stopped and two doctors came ashore. They advised sending the girl to a hospital. By six that evening, the tender *Lupine* arrived, on orders from Lighthouse District Superintendent Captain Harry Rhodes, and the child was rushed to a San Francisco hospital. After a prolonged hospitalization, the youngster recovered. The Johnsons, as had parents before them, requested a transfer to a shore station. Captain Rhodes arranged to send them to Point Loma light at San Diego. The Johnsons would spend twenty-one happy

A large wireless antenna is hauled along the little Farallon railroad. C. 1930's. (U.S. Coast Guard)

years at Point Loma, and Milford Johnson would rise to become principal keeper.

Serious medical problems such as these, including a fire in which a Navy man was fatally burned, prompted the Navy to station a pharmacist's mate on the island and to provide a greater range of medical supplies.

Interestingly, while the islanders had been inadequately supplied for their own protection, they were, from a fairly early date, equipped to respond to shipwrecks. In 1908, at the request of the Life-Saving Service, agreement was reached with the Lighthouse Service to erect a small building on Southeast Farallon to house a Lyle gun, breeches buoy, and other rescue apparatus. Keepers were trained in handling the equipment and rescue techniques. At least as late as the 1930's, this equipment was kept in readiness and drills held. This made Farallons an unusually well-prepared light station should a shipwreck occur. The wickies also acquired three small boats (the largest was 20 feet long), which might be of some use in aiding mariners.

During the years of the Great Depression, there were many happy times on the Farallons. (After all, it was one of the few places with full employment.) There were frequent parties with dancing to radio music, and playing bridge continued to be a popular pastime. The great, flat catchment basin for the cistern proved to be a fine concrete tennis court. There was the usual gardening and fishing. Some families held religious services or read the Bible on Sundays. One man managed to befriend a sea lion, and it would follow him about the station.

But the work continued to be hard. Coal arrived in 75-pound sacks and was carried on the little railroad flatcar to the coal sheds where it was stored. Families did their laundry in these sheds and coal dust made cleaning almost impossible. Painting was done regularly; and the lighthouse roof and the derrick were two of the most difficult jobs. Milford Johnson, while he was there, usually did these chores, since he had little fear of heights. In the traditional manner, a rope was tied around the ball on the lantern room roof, furnishing a good handgrip during painting. Thursday was "clean-up day," because Friday was usually "boat day" and one never knew when Captain Rhodes might arrive for inspection. Louise Johnson remembers Captain Rhodes as a "very distinguished looking man, white hair, short mustache, and usually wearing white gloves." He expected everything to be "shipshape" at the Farallons. Captain Rhodes would run his white glove over door sills and behind coal-burning stoves to make sure things were being properly maintained.

By 1935 Frank W. Ritchie was principal keeper. The *Undaunted* still served the island, and the Navy's wireless station (rechristened a radio compass station) was going strong. There was a triangle of compass stations, with one each at the Farallons, Point Reyes, and Point Montara. The fog signal now ran on compressed air instead of steam. Then, in 1939, the Coast Guard absorbed the Lighthouse Service. This change was highly significant for a civilian, family-oriented service, which allowed long-term residency. The Coast Guard represented a quasi-military organization where interchangeability of men and equipment would have priority. Still, the Coast Guard always respected the Farallons and never changed conditions significantly. In fact, the Coast Guard deserves credit for continuing to enforce strict conservation rules to protect marine and bird life on the islands.

World War II brought the greatest population increases to the islands, although the largest was a temporary one. In 1944, during thick fog, the liberty ship *Henry Bergh* rammed Southeast Farallon Island. Loaded with a thousand war-weary sailors, the badly damaged ship began to break up. Landing barges transported the sailors from the ship to the island, saving all hands. It was a record-breaking day for visitors.

After the war, the Coast Guard made an attempt at "beautifying" the island. About 1949, trees and shrubs in gallon cans were swung ashore and planted. None survived. Today, just two Monterey cypresses remain, planted years ago by the Lighthouse Service. The choice of Monterey cypress at lighthouses and lifeboat stations proved to be a wise one. The cypresses thrive at stations from Crescent City to Point Pinos. They could withstand the winds and fog at Point Reyes, Point Bonita, Arena Cove, and two dozen other stations. Farallons, however, was almost too much for the hardy trees, and only the two, in the lee of a dwelling, survive.

While the Monterey cypresses struggled in the wind, Coast Guard families of the 1950's and early 1960's continued to experience problems similar to their predecessors a half-century before. Even in the early 1960's, the Farallons station was still a family one, although families with school-age children were not assigned there, since the island lacked a teacher. The Coast Guard families stationed on the island were subject to the same maladies of young families anywhere. If a case was not serious, medical advice would be given by radio. In more

By the final decade of manned operation, the original lens had been removed and these more modern beacons placed in the lighthouse. (U.S. Coast Guard)

extreme cases, a Coast Guard patrol boat would make the run out and bring the patient into San Francisco. Helicopters occasionally rushed doctors to the island, and emergency calls had to be sent out to find a physician willing to go to the Farallons.

Having dependents on the island increased the costs of maintaining the station. Coast Guard officials eventually decided that the problems of pregnancy (expectant mothers left in the seventh month to wait on the mainland) and childhood diseases resulted in untenable transportation costs. Thus, they terminated the Farallons' status as a family station, and new people were assigned. No more would island children stand at the landing watching Christmas trees and presents be swung ashore in cargo bags by the old derrick.

After the families left in 1962, six men were assigned, with four on duty and two on leave at any one time. One of the frame dwellings was remodeled to house the men. The other residence became the home of ornithologists studying the bird population. The era of the light keepers lasted but one more decade.

After August, 1972, the light station ceased to be a fully-manned light station. The staff was reduced to two keepers who alternated duty. Only one keeper was on the island at a time. The reduced staff was made possible by complete automation. The duty primarily consisted of watching the automated generators and electronic equipment for possible malfunctions. The light, fog signal, and radio beacon all were put on continuous, 24-hour operation.

The Farallons' last keeper, Brent Franze, wrote of his life during the station's last several months as a manned facility:

> The island I live on is approximately 120 acres in size. It contains two houses, one for civilian "birdwatchers" and one for Coast Guard personnel. The island is rocky and inaccessible to boaters, as some have found out the hard way. This necessitates using a "Billy Pugh" net . . . for getting on and off the island. It is a rather exciting ride in that you are for a time suspended in the air. The landing itself is 30 feet above the water.
>
> I have all the modern conveniences (water and fuel are monthly supplied by ship) including a radio, television, pool table, washer and dryer, current magazines, and books of my choosing. I often spend time watching the seals at play or the many birds that occupy the island.

On December 1, 1972, Franze was taken off the island on the cutter *Resolute,* ending 117 years of manned operation. Resident keepers will probably never return to the Farallons. The facility is now monitored by a radio link to Coast Guard Base San Francisco on Yerba Buena Island.

However, the Farallons story does not quite end here. Scientists from the Point Reyes Bird Observatory remained on the island. The Coast Guard still must make routine maintenance runs to the island every few weeks. Because helicopters are so disturbing to the bird life, access to the island is still primarily by ship. To this day, the ancient derrick continues to swing men and women up onto the island using the time-honored Billy Pugh net. It is still quite a ride.

Leaving Farallon Islands on a Billy Pugh net, June 21, 1972. Such nets have been in use at the more dangerous offshore light stations at least since 1900. On rough days the ride is often hazardous and frightening. (R. Shanks)

A nineteenth century view of the first Point Arena lighthouse. All of the station's light-keeping families lived in the huge dwelling shown here. (Bancroft Library)

POINT ARENA AND ARENA COVE

Beyond Bodega Bay the coast is dark and lonely. For more than fifty miles there are no lighthouses and no harbors. Magnetic disturbances confuse compasses, while offshore rocks and hidden reefs are frequently cloaked in thick fog. To this day, there are but two buoys and one wharf between Bodega Bay and Point Arena. The coast trends to the northwest for these fifty miles, culminating in the sweeping headland that is Point Arena. Point Arena is but sixty feet high, low when one recalls the towering cliffs to the south. Here, too, the land changes, the rugged sheep and timber country suddenly becoming pastoral. The Coast Range mountains pull back from the sea and gentle hills with a scattering of streams and cows and villages rim the Pacific.

But if the land becomes gentle, the sea does not. Flat, treeless Point Arena reaches seaward, nearly intersecting the shipping lanes. Deep water is broken first by Arena Rock, a mile and a half off the headland, then by inshore rocks and finally by the point itself.

It was near the very tip of the point that the Lighthouse Service chose to build a 100-foot-high lighthouse. It was to be a handsome, conical, masonry tower, painted white and capped with a black lantern room with double balconies and ornamental trim. Such an isolated lighthouse did not need a flashing character, so a huge, fixed, first order lens was installed. It produced a light visible for twenty-one miles at sea. The beacon was entered at ground level through an attached, cottage-like watchroom.

Seaward of the lighthouse, at the point's extremity, was the fog signal building, a frame structure with two 12-inch steam whistles protruding from its roof. Its boiler fires would consume cordwood, sometimes burning one hundred tons during foggy years when over one thousand hours of fog annually darkened the region. The thirsty boilers needed water, too, so two, huge, underground rooms were excavated and lined with brick. The double rooms ran from one edge of the point to the other and served as cisterns.

Landward of the lighthouse stood the keepers' dwelling, a great two-and-a-half-story, brick residence which housed the entire four-man crew and all their wives and children. Beyond the dwelling was a spacious, fenced yard with well-maintained outbuildings: barn, laundry sheds, hen house, and the like, all carefully whitewashed.

On May 1, 1870, both the light and the fog whistle went into operation. The keepers immediately set about performing the timeless tasks of light keeping. Every evening began with the "light-up" watch, the first watch of the evening. During the night, each wickie would take his turn tending the light, awakening his replacement as his duties ended. During thick weather, there were also "fog watches," which meant that each keeper must stand, in addition to his watch at the lighthouse, a second watch at the fog signal. Double watches sometimes resulted in attendants working sixteen hours in twenty-four.

The nightly watches were in addition to the routine work done during the day. There was, for example, the usual painting, from oil room floor to the smokestacks of the fog signal. There was cleaning (especially the brasswork in the lighthouse) and the constant picking up, particularly about the woodpile adjacent to the fog signal. The lantern room and lens atop the sentinel was a particular chore. Inside the lens was a large reservoir which had to be continually filled with oil for the beacon's lamp. If the reservoir was overfilled, the oil would spill out, spattering the spotless lens and floors. Inside the lamp, the burner often needed to be changed or the wicks trimmed. Less common, but nevertheless time-consuming, chores included replacing the reservoir or even drilling out the corroded bolts on the lantern room door hinges and installing new ones.

The first Point Arena lighthouse was flanked by the dwelling and the fog signal building (at right). C. 1896. (Robert J. Lee)

Life was not all work, however. The new station's keepers found that the area offered fine abalone hunting and, seasonally, salmon spearing. Whenever the supply of fish ran low, neighbor "Fisherman Frank" would happily share his catch. If a keeper could get one of the other wickies to stand his watch, there was an occasional ball held nearby in the town of Point Arena. When no ball was scheduled, the town saloon offered diversion; although one or two keepers were known to overstay their visit, and "returned with their keg pretty well filled," the log noted. However, most pleasures were simple and confined to the station: greeting wagonloads of guests on visitors day or chatting with the tinner as he repaired a roof.

Light keeping meant constant responsibility and unending interaction with others living at the station. Life could be awfully confining at an isolated light station; and with Point Arena's single residence, privacy was minimal. The big dwelling was filled with adults and children. The walls were thick, but the floors were not. An old lady's rocking chair could echo down to a bedroom below where an assistant keeper desperately tried to sleep after long watches. Children yelled, ran, cried, and played tricks, much to the annoyance of some less tolerant keepers. One keeper's wife annoyed her peers by using the fine linen "tower towels" (supplied to clean the lens) as diapers for her baby. Sometimes keepers became frustrated with the monotony and the strain of early-day light keeping. According to the log, one wickie spent the day singing, "acting the fool," and staring in windows trying to annoy the first assistant. When the lighthouse began its second decade of operation in January, 1880, first assistant keeper George Koons summed it all up when he logged: "threatening weather and fighting children."

The weather was much worse than the children. The wind, particularly, was fierce. During the winter of 1879-80, all the fences were blown down. On February 26, 1880, the "worst gale ever seen" hit the station. The wind hurled everything movable in all directions; even wheelbarrows flew through the air.

A month later, during a "perfect gale," word reached the harried and underpaid keepers that there would be a "reduction of . . . salaries," a move keeper Koons greeted with the grim recognition that the wickies were, in his opinion, already living at near "starvation" level.

However, it was not always a case of too much wind and too little money at Point Arena. Sometimes there was no wind at all. During such calm spells, "the heaviest kind of black fog" would creep in. Then the boilers in the fog signal building had to be fired up. If the water was cold, it would take thirty-five minutes to build up steam sufficient to blow the whistles. Sometimes, however, the water would still be warm from the previous day and sufficient steam pressure could be had in as little as eight minutes.

This was all well and good, except that steam, of course, requires a lot of water. A windmill was used to pump water from the cistern to the fog signal. Since fog often coincided with windless weather, there was a constant worry that the station would run out of water and the whistles would stop issuing their warning blasts. However, Point Arena's luck held and, although they once were down to a day's supply, the station apparently never ran out of water. Happily, the light ended its first decade with no more than the routine happenings of the time: principal keeper George Brennan bought a cow from Fisherman Frank; first assistant Koons continued to help his wife with the laundry; Mrs. Brennan went off to have a baby; and the sash cord the government sent out for the fog signal ended up as a clothesline. But then a frightening thing happened.

June 7, 1880, Koons was on watch in the light tower. At 1:15 a.m. he heard a very heavy rumbling, things began to rattle all about him, and he suddenly felt the "very sharp shock" of an earthquake. Koons was quite shaken and, fearing more tremors, left the tower. He reported to keeper Brennan, who was on watch in the fog signal building, just a few yards away. Reaching the fog signal, Koons was stunned to learn that Brennan had not even felt the quake. This, despite the fact that the San Andreas fault runs just off the point.

The lighthouse had shown its alarming vulnerability to earthquakes; a tremor not even felt in the frame fog signal building had seriously shaken the brick light tower. When Koons received orders transferring him to East Brother lighthouse on San Francisco Bay, he had few regrets upon leaving Point Arena.

Koons, Brennan, and their fellows had, however, achieved a fine record at Point Arena, for that year the lighthouse inspector pronounced the station "the best on the coast."

The last two decades of the nineteenth century saw many improvements at the station. The road was rebuilt, a telephone line was constructed to the hotel in town where the phone company was headquartered, Kentucky bluegrass seed was cast about the station, and Monterey cypress seedlings arrived aboard the tender *Madroño*.

The fog, wind, and sea all combined to make Point Arena a dangerous place for mariners. By 1900 it had become clear that the lighthouse would have to be supplemented by a life-saving station. Since the lighting of the beacon, there had been at least thirteen major shipwrecks at or near the point. The sentinel could make the sea lanes safer, but it could never overcome all hazards.

Three miles to the south of the light there was a fine cove with a small, rocky beach protected by high cliffs. Here, on May 6, 1903, the

Ruins of the 1st Arena Light House March 2d 07

After the 1906 earthquake the original lighthouse was demolished and this temporary lighthouse was constructed. 1907. (Robert J. Lee)

U.S. Life-Saving Service established its Arena Cove Life-Saving Station. The cove offered the only real shelter in over fifty miles of coastline. It was secure enough to allow a wharf to be built so that steam schooners might tie up to load lumber. More importantly, as far as the Life-Saving Service was concerned, the beach offered enough protection that a boathouse and launchways could be constructed without having to fear that they would be washed out every winter by storms. The boathouse held a lifeboat and a surfboat. Back from the beach and up the hill was the solid, frame station itself. High on the bluff south of the cove, with an incredible view of the sea, stood a red-roofed lookout tower on steel supports, which assured coastwise sailors that any sign of trouble would be noticed.

Landlubbers were impressed as well. That first Fourth of July, the life-saving station keeper and his crew of eight surfmen hitched up their team to the boat carriage. They then hauled the surfboat down the main street of the little town of Point Arena in the parade. They topped the day with a breeches buoy demonstration, attracting a large crowd. Lacking a well-timed shipwreck, the surfmen had to be content with "saving" one of their own from a dead tree.

The breeches buoy demonstration was to pale before the events of April 18, 1906. The great earthquake that was to leave San Francisco in ruins—and to destroy the town of Point Arena as well—hit the brick lighthouse with tremendous force. When the shaking ended, the lighthouse still stood; but it was shattered beyond repair, with cracks and holes in its walls. The first order lens was wrecked. The big dwelling was a total loss, and the families were without shelter. Tents had to be pitched, and everyone prepared for the worst. They did not have to wait long. A large, crazed black bear soon appeared and began running around the station. The wickies had had trouble with bears before and some routinely packed guns for protection. The crazed bear, like the lighthouse, ended its career beside the fog signal building.

Given the destruction of their residence and the obvious inadequacies of tents on such a windy point, the keepers found that they had no choice but to move into the little, frame outbuildings that survived. The Lighthouse Service, required to await Congressional funding, had but limited funds to cope with a disaster which ranged from Point Pinos to Cape Mendocino. The local wickies would see hard times for the remainder of the year. The Lighthouse Service could do little more than urge its employees to "make yourselves reasonably comfortable temporarily" in the sheds and to "proceed without further authority with what is absolutely necessary, reporting all liabilities incurred." Giving keepers such freedom in purchasing needed materials was almost unheard of in the frugal Lighthouse Service. Such an extreme departure from procedure illustrates the severe blow the 1906 earthquake had dealt normal operations. It wouldn't be until October that year—six months after the earthquake—that construction superintendent Samuel Hooke would set out from San Francisco to begin work on four new cottages for Point Arena's wickies.

The keepers struggled to restore normal operations. The navigational aids had to be restored, particularly since lumber schooners loaded with wood to rebuild San Francisco moved by the point in increasing numbers. Fortunately, the fog signal building, being of wood, had survived the quake. The lighthouse, while still standing precariously, represented a serious problem. First, its lantern room had to be removed from the tower, no small task since it was one hundred feet in the air atop a building rent with cracks and holes.

The lantern room was eventually removed safely and reinstalled atop a wood skeleton tower (complete with a lamp-cleaning room) built nearby. A second order lens was requisitioned for the emergency, and on January 5, 1907, the temporary lighthouse began operation. The fog signal building, relatively undamaged, was also in operation again. The station had been so badly damaged that it had taken the Lighthouse Service over eight months to restore normal operations.

The new Point Arena lighthouse nears completion. Note that the broad base housing the buttresses has yet to be added. (Robert J. Lee)

Other tasks had been proceeding apace. By December, 1906, the old dwelling had been dismantled. By March, 1907, the old light tower had been reduced to a mere stub. Unsalvageable materials were cast over the cliff into the sea and the point was cleaned of debris.

However, a serious engineering problem remained—how to build a new lighthouse capable of withstanding another major earthquake. Engineers decided to make a radical departure from traditional masonry or stone construction techniques. A company specializing in construction of tall, concrete chimneys for industry was hired to build the new beacon. The chimney company began by constructing a 115-foot-high light tower, utilizing scaffolding which completely surrounded the sentinel and eventually rose more than one hundred feet in the air. By late November, 1907, scaffolding was beginning to come down, revealing the first reinforced concrete lighthouse in the United States. It was a feat that was to forever alter lighthouse construction. New Canadian lighthouses and modern Coast Guard automatic structures to this day are both commonly made of reinforced concrete. Point Arena's vulnerability to earthquakes required, however, that something more be added; massive cement buttresses, enclosed in a cylindrical room more than twice the diameter of the tower, were erected at the base of the beacon. The completed lighthouse stood, gleaming white with a black lantern room, like a statue on a pedestal. Here was a lighthouse truly adapted to California's earthquake country.

The Lighthouse Service had to create almost an entirely new light station after the destructive 1906 earthquake. Note the four cottages that replaced the original single dwelling. C. 1930's. (U.S. Coast Guard)

The new, first order, flashing lens was as interesting as the innovative buttresses. It actually floated on a bath of mercury. The lens rested on a short, vertical shaft which extended into a broad, enclosed tub. The shaft had a horizontal plate at its lower end which floated atop the mercury in the tub. When the clockwork-drive system rotated the lens, the floating shaft provided a virtually frictionless method of rotation. The lens was balanced so precisely that anyone entering the lens had to first tighten several small supports or the lens would tip like a boat in water. On January 15, 1908, the lamp was lighted, and keeper Robert H. Williams and his three assistants placed the new beacon in operation.

They not only had a new lighthouse, but new dwellings as well. Four cottages had been built to replace the older single residence. The new houses were comfortable and afforded increased privacy, factors which led Point Arena to become an increasingly popular station at which to serve.

The coming decade saw a well-organized, functioning station. Keeper Williams had the road improved, using six horses to pull the scraper and four more on the roller. In 1916, Williams received special recognition from the Lighthouse Service because he had been alert in spotting a disabled launch about to drift into nearby breakers. Williams had used the special telephone line that connected the lighthouse with the Arena Cove Lifeboat Station to notify the Coast Guard, and in short order, all were saved.

During the late 1920's a mysterious boatman appeared one day, off the light. The stranger wanted to come ashore, so the wickies directed him down to Arena Cove, where a safe landing was possible. The man was unfamiliar with the coast and unknown to local residents, yet here he was in a small boat. One persistent rumor held that a ship, with a substantial sum of money on board, had sunk offshore and that the uncommunicative stranger was connected with it. But like the dissipating fog, the lone boatman quickly vanished from the bluffs of Point Arena.

In 1932, a very different kind of man arrived at the station. It was young Wayne Piland, reporting for his first assignment in the Lighthouse Service. The Depression was on, and it had taken Piland 13 months of waiting to receive his appointment. He was no stranger to the Lighthouse Service; he had been in the Navy; his stepfather had served in Alaska aboard the lighthouse tender *Cedar;* and his wife's uncle had been a keeper on the Farallon Islands. Besides the usual duties, Piland was immediately placed in charge of the station windmill. It was his duty to assure that the redwood tanks were constantly full of water. There was plenty of wind and water that year, and windmill duty was a simple introduction to light keeping.

Then one day, Captain Rhodes arrived for inspection. Harry Rhodes had been District Superintendent of all the lights in California since 1912, a post he would hold until his retirement in 1939. Captain Rhodes was a no-nonsense man, brilliant, completely autocratic, precise, thorough, and incredibly frugal. He was, Piland recalls, "a man with whom you stood up straight and were careful with what you said." Rhodes "didn't take sass from anyone," and he ruled his district with an iron hand. When the lighthouse tender steamed into Arena Cove with the superintendent's flag flying, you could bet that he'd expect to find everything spotless, from the top of the lens to the rear of the kitchen stove. Captain Rhodes wore white gloves and ran them over doorsills looking for dust. Rhodes was known, and feared, from Point Loma to Crescent City.

Captain Rhodes' frugality was legendary. If something wore out, it was not just thrown away. Piland and keeper "Win" Kane were in the tool room inside the fog signal building during one inspection when Captain Rhodes spied a worn-out broom Kane had planned to throw out. "What's the matter with this?" the superintendent demanded. Kane tried to explain, "Captain Rhodes, this broom is just worn out." Rhodes cut him short, "Why, this could still be used for scraping whitewash off a fence. Put it back in service." Rhodes then saw a can opener with the blade broken off. Kane commented that he planned to discard it too, since it could no longer be used to open cans. Rhodes responded, "Well, the corkscrew on it is all right. It could still be used for opening a bottle. And I don't mean a bottle of wine!" Rhodes then set Piland to work filing old screwdrivers back into shape.

Piland felt the full impact of the Service's attempts to cut costs when, after six months, his third assistant's position was eliminated and he was transferred to Humboldt Bay. Point Arena would often be short-handed during the coming years.

While exacting inspections were typical of all California stations, Point Arena was fairly unusual in that much of the work had to be done at great heights. Each spring Robert Williams would have his men rig a pulley and pull him up and down the light tower while he did the dangerous task of painting. His successor, Win Kane, was not afraid of heights either. Once Kane was working high atop one of the big water tanks, directing a contractor and his crew as they replaced some timbers. Apparently, the over-zealous crew removed one timber too many, as suddenly the tank collapsed, hurtling thirty feet to the ground. Both tank and keeper went down; mercifully, it was the tank and not Kane that ended up in little pieces. The keeper limped away with only a sprained ankle.

In 1937, Point Arena came under the command of Bill Owens. Owens had served as assistant keeper at both Point Sur and Point Con-

Captain Harry W. Rhodes, Superintendent of the 18th Lighthouse District from 1912 until 1939. Captain Rhodes was in charge of all of California's lighthouses and lightships. In this rare photo, he stands on the bridge of the lighthouse tender Sequoia *during the 1930's. (U.S. Coast Guard)*

Arena Cove Life-Saving Station. C. 1908. (Robert J. Lee)

Surfboat on the launchways at Arena Cove Life-Saving Station's boathouse. C. 1904. (Robert J. Lee)

ception, two of the south coast's most rugged stations. With him was his wife Isabel and their children. He and his family were eager for their new life at Point Arena.

The family soon settled into their new routine. Owens began standing the long watches in the fog signal building, alert to start the five-foot-tall generators which now provided electricity for the light and powered the compressed-air fog horns. While Mr. Owens had the benefits of electricity for the navigational aids, the frugal Lighthouse Service provided no electricity for the dwellings. Isabel Owens still had to light coal-oil lamps and wash with washboard and buckets.

There was plenty to do at Point Arena. There were four-hour watches each night, maintenance work during the day, a "Visitors Day" on Saturday and Sunday afternoons from one to four o'clock, and the like. Every Saturday morning was lens-cleaning time, a two-hour chore. Many were the days when Bill Owens would crawl into bed after eighteen or twenty hours' work.

Sometimes he worked longer. During that first year, Owens found himself incredibly shorthanded. While one assistant keeper was away on vacation, another had to be relieved of his duties, and a third keeper simply decided he had had enough of light keeping and left. When the fog rolled in, Bill and Isabel Owens found themselves with a four-man light station on their hands and no qualified people to help them. So they operated it alone.

Unlike the assistant keepers, the fog stayed. For two days and nights, Owens went without sleep, fully aware that human lives depended upon his light and horn. Then, about 2 a.m. on the third day, the exhausted Owens went out to oil the generators and air compressors in the fog signal building. He staggered into the building and collapsed from exhaustion. He regained consciousness long enough to call his wife. Isabel Owens, with six young children to care for, was the only other person with the knowledge and skill to operate the equipment. She relieved her husband and stood watch through the night.

At dawn, Owens knew something had to be done. He telephoned Captain Rhodes in San Francisco, telling him that he couldn't carry on without help and that his wife was taking him to a doctor. Owens demanded assistance. The superintendent only balked for a moment. Owens threatened to leave the station unattended if he weren't immediately authorized to hire a temporary assistant. Rhodes agreed and a young ranch-hand was employed. Isabel Owens taught the ranch-hand how to run the machinery, and they continued to operate the station until Owens could get back on his feet. Owens recovered and resumed his grinding schedule, but it was three months before permanent assistants were provided.

By 1938, Owens had a full, well-trained crew under his command.

Arena Cove's eight surfmen and the station keeper (at right) with the beach apparatus. The crew harnessed themselves to the beach cart and pulled it to shipwrecks. July 4, 1904. (Robert J. Lee)

They were certainly needed. That year a fishing boat, a big purse seiner, went ashore on the beach just to the north, at the mouth of the Garcia River. Then, a short while later, a steamer hit Saunders Reef to the south. Arena Cove's 36-foot motor lifeboat sped to the scene and saved all on board. Coast Guardsmen then returned to attempt to save the ship. They managed to get a towline on her, but suddenly a big wave hit the damaged vessel and her bow plunged toward the bottom. A Coast Guardsman in the stern of the motor lifeboat cut the towline to keep from being pulled under, and the salvage operation ended.

The ship was gone, but not her cargo. Cans of coffee floated all over the sea. Unlike many cargos, the coffee did not come ashore. So the local people got into their boats and acquired coffee at all-time low prices.

The 1930's ended and with them the Lighthouse Service. The Coast Guard assumed control of the light in 1939. It was a new outfit with different values than the old Lighthouse Service. The day he was inducted into the Coast Guard, Owens climbed the light's circular stairs with a can of paint in his hand. He began his work, and when he had finished, the gleaming brasswork of the lens had been painted a military gray. The end of the Lighthouse Service was a blow to many of the great keepers, and there was bitterness at many light stations that summer. Among light-keeping families even today not all of the pain is gone.

Although the Coast Guard had, by Presidential action, absorbed the Lighthouse Service, the light stations continued to be staffed by the same personnel. The keepers now came under the command of Coast Guard officers, whose knowledge of lighthouses was generally inferior to their own. The transition had mixed reviews. Where thoughtful Coast Guard officers realized the expertise of the old-time keepers, the wickies were cooperative and instructive, patiently explaining their station's operation. Less perceptive officers, interested more in asserting their authority than in gaining competency in their command, sometimes made foolish decisions and increased mistrust. At one light station, for instance, the new Coast Guard inspector ordered all tool handles stamped with the initials of the Lighthouse Service to be removed, broken, and replaced with handles bearing Coast Guard lettering. This was a far cry from the traditions established by Captain Rhodes and his predecessors.

Fortunately, such officers were in the minority. Further, the Coast Guard was much more generous with supplies than the frugal Lighthouse Service. The principal, long-term problem which resulted from Coast Guard control was that enlisted men served such short tours of duty at light stations that it became difficult for old-time keepers to adequately train their assistants. Eventually, the skill level at some light stations declined significantly, and the Coast Guard came to depend upon highly skilled specialists from San Francisco or Humboldt Bay to perform the more difficult maintenance and repair work.

Whatever the merits of civilian, as opposed to Coast Guard, administration, Point Arena continued under Bill Owens to function as a highly efficient station. Then there occurred an event much more far-reaching than the demise of the Lighthouse Service.

In December, 1941, the Japanese attacked Pearl Harbor and America became involved in World War II. During the following days, the light station was especially alert. One morning, Owens was on watch as day was breaking. Isabel Owens was up early too, working in the kitchen. Then, just west of the fog signal building, they both saw something rise from the sea. It was a Japanese submarine! The submarine surfaced, two Asians stuck their heads out of the hatch, looked around, and then quickly closed the hatch. The submarine immediately submerged, heading north. Owens rushed to phone the Navy headquarters in San Francisco. But the Navy man on duty was unimpressed with Owens' sighting.

Keeper Owens Pt. Arena Light C[?]

The legendary Bill Owens, keeper of Point Arena lighthouse, surveys the coast from the lighthouse balcony. Note the handgrips along the vertical window frames. The handgrips prevent keepers from being blown off the tower when cleaning the windows during high winds. (Bill and Isabel Owens)

"There are no Japanese submarines in this country," he stated authoritatively. He counseled Owens to "go back to bed."

Not many days later, off Cape Mendocino, the American tanker *Emidio* was torpedoed, victim of a Japanese submarine attack. Two days later the newspapers published pictures of Japanese submarines. One was identical to the vessel the Owens had seen.

World War II meant that the radio beacon was reduced to a ten-mile range, so that only coasting vessels could use it. The light, however, never went dark. Even during blackouts, when the keepers' dwellings were darkened, the great light continued to shine. When all the coast was dark in anticipation of a possible enemy attack, it was quite a feeling to be sitting at the base of the only light to be glowing in seventy-five miles of coastline.

The war meant that a record number of people came to live at the point. The reality of Japanese military operations along the coast was no longer in doubt, and the Coast Guard established its famed "Beach Patrol" all along the California coast. Everyone doubled up at Point Arena light station as enlisted men moved into one of the dwellings. The young Coast Guardsmen manned a lookout station at the light (located near the fog signal building) and patrolled beaches and headlands north and south of the light. They were but one small link in a network that covered hundreds of miles of coastline so that even the most isolated cove was watched.

During the war, too, nature darkened the skies more pervasively than any blackout ever could. A gigantic forest fire broke out in the timberlands, and from it a blanket of smoke arose, covering much of the Mendocino Coast. For seventeen days and nights the air was so thick that the fog signal had to be run constantly.

Smoke was not the only thing in the air. One clear day Owens saw a big Navy blimp coming up the coast from the south. He watched fascinated as it seemed to head directly toward the lighthouse. The closer the airship got, the more it seemed to be aiming at the light. By now, the blimp was so low that Owens could see people on board. As the dirigible neared the lighthouse, it was lower than the tower itself. Then, with a glancing blow, the blimp hit the lighthouse, its side scraping the tower just below the lantern room. The blimp bounced off and continued on up the coast. It may well have been the only case in history of a blimp-lighthouse collision.

A more tragic error occurred when several military planes ran out of fuel over the point. One plane crashed just offshore, and Owens and his crew attempted to salvage the plane. They rushed to the scene, swimming the Garcia River to reach the plane. Once there, they worked until one o'clock in the morning, often in water up to their necks, trying to get the plane out of the sea and up on the beach.

The end of World War II meant that Point Arena again became the home of just the four lighthouse keepers and their families. Many navigational aids had been improved during the war, but Point Arena remained a great danger to mariners.

On a foggy morning of September 9, 1949, Bill and Isabel Owens were having breakfast. They could hear a freighter coming down the coast, its fog horn blowing. Soon it sounded, as Mrs. Owens described it, "like the ship was right in our backyard." Owens headed for the fog signal building to get a better look. Before he reached the signal, he heard the unmistakable sound of the ship hitting Arena Rock. Grabbing the telephone, he alerted the Arena Cove lifeboat station and then called Coast Guard headquarters in San Francisco. The Coast Guard response was swift. The Arena Cove 36-foot motor lifeboat sped to the scene and big cutters were dispatched from San Francisco Bay. The motor lifeboat arrived off the point in minutes. Her crew found the British freighter *Pacific Enterprise* stranded on the offshore rocks. The lifeboat crew took off some of those on board, but most of the ship's crew stayed with the vessel as there was hope of saving her. Later, the big Coast Guard cutters arrived, but there was little they could do to assist the heavily damaged freighter. At last, everyone left the ship. It took the Pacific a little over a week to pound the ship to pieces. The light keepers watched as the ship broke in half. Then the aft section went down, followed a few days later by the bow.

Bill and Isabel Owens stayed at the light until 1952. Some evenings they would take out the ancient log book and read of the lives of their predecessors. There were happy things, such as the time when a couple was married high in the lighthouse lantern room. And sad times, as when an epidemic swept the town of Point Arena, and each day the station would send a keeper into town to help care for the sick. And even things to make one shudder, as when they read of a third assistant keeper disappearing into the great blowhole in front of the fog signal building. The wickies called the huge pit "Devil's Punchbowl," and the Owens recalled one of their more adventuresome daughters climbing down into the blowhole. Then the Owens family was transferred up the coast to Point Cabrillo, and the station lost its last civilian keeper.

The Coast Guardsmen ran the station during the 1960's and 1970's. It continued to be one of the best-run and best-maintained stations in California. Much of the old-time tradition lasted into the late 1970's. Even in these recent years, the keepers have rescued people from the cliffs. When emergency generators failed to operate during a power failure, the keepers ran the ancient lens using oil lamps and the old clockwork drive powered by a massive weight.

The Coast Guardsmen once even got a taste of old-time light-keeping problems. On one of those occasions when they were using the clockwork drive, the wire rope that held the weight broke. The weight shot down the tower, crashed through the thick steel cap at the bottom of the drop tube, and dented the concrete floor. Every ghost in the tower must have had an opinion about that accident. Perhaps they had a hand in it.

The great lens still floats in mercury, although on rare occasions it gets stuck and rotates poorly. In the past, Bill Owens has been called from his retirement in a cottage at Little River to repair this problem. He has willingly returned, carefully opening up each side of the tub at the lens' base. Then he would pull a tongue depressor from his pocket and gently remove the little dust balls that had accumulated on top of the mercury. Once these were removed, the lens again worked per-fectly. The Owens then would drive from the station, past the twin concrete oil houses, beyond the four new keepers' dwellings, and out the gate. That evening, a Coast Guardsman would pull the curtain along its rod, revealing the lens. Then he would turn on the light and the lens would begin revolving. It was a priceless moment to experience.

Point Arena lighthouse may be seen by driving north 1-3/4 miles from the town of Point Arena. Turn left on Lighthouse Road and drive about one and a half miles to reach the station. A fine view can be had just south of the station. With automation having occurred in June, 1977, visiting hours are uncertain. Hopefully, the Coast Guard, together with a responsible group such as the Mendocino County Historical Society, will work to open the station to the public. Along with the beautiful lighthouse itself, the visitor will see one of the finest fog signal buildings on the Pacific Coast, complete with paneled walls, grandfather clocks, and other interesting equipment. The station deserves both careful preservation and frequent visitors.

Point Arena lighthouse showing the broad base which houses the earthquake-resistant buttresses. The fog signal building adjacent to the lighthouse was all that survived the 1906 earthquake. 1975. (R. Shanks)

Historic Point Cabrillo lighthouse is architecturally unique. Twin air sirens can be seen atop the beacon's roof. C. 1915. (Robert J. Lee)

POINT CABRILLO

Point Cabrillo was the light of the steam schooners, those fearless little lumber ships that plied the "doghole" ports of the Mendocino Coast. It is still the sentinel of the commercial fishermen and of coastal freighters. It is a beautiful light station where time has stood still.

At Point Cabrillo, the land and sea become a part of each other. The Pacific surges up inlets on both sides of the lighthouse. Even on moderate days the exposed position of the station is evident as the ocean rushes in and explodes with such force that spray reaches well above the sixty-foot-high cliffs. The wind then takes the tops off the spray and drops of salty rain fall upon the lighthouse. The sea thus becomes a part of the air, the mist blowing about the flat headland with its carpet of wildflowers and hedgerow of cypresses.

Over a dozen ships have met their doom between the neighboring ports of Caspar and Mendocino City. Not only coastwise shipping, but the lumber vessels using many nearby coves needed a guidepost. The need was most acute during easterly and northerly weather when these ships hugged the shore, depending on the lee of the land as protection from wind and sea. In 1909, as a response to the local lumber trade, Point Cabrillo Light Station was built. Carpenters, teams and wagons swarmed about the headland, constructing a dozen buildings. It was to be a true lumber-country beacon with every structure—save the concrete oil house—built of wood.

Almost the entire station was built in a single line, at a right angle to the sea. Closest to the ocean was the lighthouse, a unique octagonal tower, 47 feet high, with an attached fog signal room on the seaward side. The completed sentinel, finished with handsome siding, looked much like a country church, except that the lantern room stood in place of a steeple. The lantern room had a single balcony and held a jewel-like third order lens. The lens was mounted atop four tiers of brass pillars and rotated on ball bearings. The wooden stairs in the tower were steep, resembling ship's ladders. The largest portion of the lighthouse was the spacious fog signal room that held the gas engines and air compressors for the twin sirens that protruded from the room's roof. The entire structure presented a colorful appearance, with black lantern room, red roof, white walls, and gray trim.

The next building landward of the lighthouse was the concrete oil house, a small, flat-roofed structure used to store kerosene, paint, and other flammable liquids. Since the Lighthouse Service had converted its lamps to kerosene, it was no longer considered safe to store oil inside

Point Cabrillo lighthouse under construction. 1909. (U.S. Coast Guard)

the lighthouse. Cement or rock oil houses thereafter became a necessity.

Beyond the oil house were the carpenter shop and blacksmith shop, both housed in one building. Wickies were expected to do most repair work themselves, be it metal or wood work. The navigational aids had to be kept going, storm damage repaired immediately, horses must be shod, windows replaced, and new cabinets built. The station had to have all the tools and materials necessary to remain independent and fully operational for several weeks or months at a time.

East of the blacksmith-carpenter building, three dwellings were built, all in a row, extending away from the sea. The principal keeper's residence was in the center and was perhaps a bit fancier than the other houses. All three were handsome, substantial homes, two stories high, with porches, brick fireplaces, and basements. There were large fenced yards, front and back. In the rear, beyond the gardens, were three fancy sheds, one for each family. Built in a style to match the architecture of the dwellings, each of these buildings served a light-keeping family as a granary, storehouse, coal house, and workshop—all in one. Behind the sheds was the pump house, cistern, and water tank. To the south, some distance away from the dwellings, was the barn, shared by all. There was nothing compact about Point Cabrillo, it was far-flung and pastoral.

On June 10, 1909, the station was complete and the lamp was lighted for the first time. It was most likely lighted by keeper Wilhelm Baumgartner. There must have been a bit of summer fog that evening, because the keepers cranked up the gasoline engines with their huge belts connected to air compressors and the fog sirens began their warning screams.

The three keepers had a choice station. Save for some heavy fog and occasional storms, Point Cabrillo boasted fine weather. Schools, churches, and stores were close by and the roads were satisfactory. There was plenty of water and good soil for farming. This was to become one of the most popular stations in the Lighthouse Service, particularly for families with school-age children. Assistant keeper Harry Miller had certainly been grateful when he arrived in 1935, after seven years at windy, fog-bound Point Sur light. Point Cabrillo was ideal for him and his family. Each keeper was allowed three cows, several pigs, and all the

The combination blacksmith shop and carpenter shop was an important building at Point Cabrillo. Many light stations had such structures, but today only this one remains in all of California. 1909. (U.S. Coast Guard)

chickens he wanted. Before long, Miller had four hundred fryers cluck-ing in his backyard. If one got tired of chicken, there was game in the hills and fish from the sea. The barn served as a slaughterhouse, and venison and ham hung in the basements of the dwellings. South of the light, there was a boom used to lower a skiff for offshore fishing. Backyards yielded a bounty of vegetables and fruit. Latticework and trellises supported flowers and vines.

Point Cabrillo did have a special hazard. Its high cliffs sometimes became quite soft, for as much as fifteen feet from the edge. Occasion-ally, a cow or horse strayed too close, the cliff gave way and the animal fell into the sea. One fortunate cow survived and keepers went in after her. They swam her through the surf and led her ashore and up the cliff, using grain as an enticement.

The usual maintenance work of painting, fence-building, roofing, and cabinet-making was similar to any other light station. Cement work, however, had one advantage at Point Cabrillo; gravel from the beach was perfect for making concrete. A little incline railway had been built down the cliff north of the lighthouse during construction of the station to haul gravel up for floors, basements, and walks. Later, it was replaced by stairs, but the beach continued to be used as a source of building materials.

As with all the light stations, there were long watches to be stood; every night for the light, and around the clock during thick weather when the fog signal was operating. Watches were six or eight hours long, and they were spent at the lighthouse in the little watch room that is on the south side of the entrance. Periodically, the man on duty would check the light or step outside to look for fast-approaching fog. (Point Cabrillo was one of those stations which could log over 1,000 hours of fog annually.) Generally, there was plenty of time to just sit at the desk and read the *Saturday Evening Post* by the table lamp. Those serene evenings are among Harry Miller's fondest memories.

In 1939 Thomas Atkinson became head keeper after having spent his earlier years at such lonely posts as St. George Reef and the Faral-lons. He was a dedicated, hard-working keeper, remembered as a kind and gentle man. He once saved Harry Miller's life.

The basements in the dwellings had been repeatedly flooded, and Miller and Atkinson were determined to dig a deep trench behind the houses to allow the seepage to drain into the ocean. It was necessarily a deep trench, and at about six feet down the men encountered unstable, watery sand. They continued digging, anyway. Miller was in the trench as they reached a depth of eight feet. Suddenly, the first assistant found himself sinking into the sand, unable to lift his feet. A moment later, the entire trench began caving in on Miller. Atkinson had already per-ceived what was happening. Instantaneously, he reached down and

Point Cabrillo was a spacious and pastoral light station, a favorite of light-keeping families. Dwellings are at right. The entire station remains unchanged today. C. 1930's. (U.S. Coast Guard)

grabbed his partner. Miller's boots resisted, but miraculously his feet slipped out and Atkinson pulled him away from a sandy grave. The boots still lie buried in the yard behind the center dwelling.

The advent of World War II was to make the watches less peaceful than previously, especially during the early months of the conflict when Japanese submarines prowled the West Coast. The Coast Guard Beach Patrol was set up to guard hundreds of lonely miles of California shore. The Beach Patrol usually made their rounds using horses or jeeps, a significant advantage over the "sandpounders" of the early Life-Saving Service patrols, who once walked the coast on foot looking for ship-wrecks. The operation was similar, however, and lookout towers and barracks were placed at regular intervals along the coast, often at exist-ing lifeboat or light stations. Point Cabrillo was one of the sites selec-ted, and soon over a dozen men were manning a lookout tower or patrolling the beaches and headlands.

Fears of Japanese spies landing along the Pacific Coast made things a bit jumpy at Point Cabrillo. Keepers began taking their hunting rifles with them when they stood watch alone at the lighthouse. One night, Harry Miller was relaxing in the watch room. During his spare moments, Miller had made a few improvements in the lighthouse. He had added a built-in medicine cabinet in the lavatory, and in the watch room he had installed a small windowpane that opened like a door to allow fresh air to come in. Suddenly, Miller was shocked to see an Asiatic-looking hand by the little window. He grabbed his rifle, but pulled himself together long enough to use the direct telephone to the dwellings. He told his two fellow keepers that there seemed to be some trouble down at the lighthouse and that they had better come fast. Miller also suggested that they bring their rifles.

Seeing his co-workers appear with rifles at the ready, Miller charged out of the lighthouse door, ready to blast the invader back to Japan. Sure enough, someone was there, but fortuitously, Miller was a man who looked before he shot. There on the ground sat a young Indian woman, the daughter of a neighbor. She had come to the lighthouse seeking help in finding her way home. Thus ended the battle for Point Cabrillo.

In January, 1952, William "Bill" Owens transferred from Point Arena to succeed Thomas Atkinson as head keeper. He would be the last civilian to serve at either station. By this time, changes had occurred at the station. Farming was no longer practiced, and the old sirens had given way to a pair of diaphone fog horns.

Just as the light stations had changed, so too had the type of distress calls the Coast Guard received. Large ships stranding at Point Arena had become a rarity, but large numbers of fishing boats still ran into trouble. Most of the fishing boats were from Noyo harbor, to the north of Point Cabrillo, near the town of Fort Bragg. This meant a delay of several hours while the Arena Cove 36-foot motor lifeboat came north to anwer a rescue call. The Coast Guard decided, therefore, to close Arena Cove Lifeboat Station. A mooring was obtained in Noyo harbor, and the motor lifeboat began serving mariners from there. Later, it became apparent that a larger patrol boat was needed to cover a territory that ran from Fish Rocks in Sonoma County north to Shelter Cove. An 83-foot patrol boat was stationed here, later to be replaced by an "82-footer." Thus, larger and faster boats with greater towing capacity, a longer cruising range, and better accommodations for the crew became the mainstay of Coast Guard search and rescue operations.* With rescue boats on the Mendocino coast now moored at Noyo, Bill Owens found that he could count on a quick response to calls for assistance at Point Cabrillo.

---

*A similar change later occurred at the Bodega Bay Coast Guard Station during the 1970's, since the station had similar calls and conditions to Noyo. Work in heavy surf has also required that a 44-foot motor lifeboat be retained there. Recently, a 25-foot motor surfboat was added at Noyo for surf work.

The storm of February, 1960 was the worst Point Cabrillo experienced. This aerial photograph was taken after conditions had subsided somewhat, yet the sea is still a complete mass of breaking white water. (U.S. Coast Guard)

Battered Point Cabrillo lighthouse immediately after the February, 1960 storm ended. Notice that the heavy doors have been smashed in, siding torn away, and windows broken. (U.S. Coast Guard)

Owens always kept an eye on the sea. During the 1950's he had spotted a commercial fishing boat drifting onto the rocks off the light. It appeared as though no one was on board. A call to Noyo brought the patrol boat in time to get a line on the fishing boat before it was destroyed in the breakers. A boarding party found that the boat was not abandoned at all. The hapless fisherman had gotten his arm caught in some machinery and was trapped on his own boat.

On another occasion there was even less time to effect a rescue. One day Owens saw smoke and, grabbing his binoculars, he could see a commercial fishing boat afire. This time he could see the crew. Two men were in the water, hanging from the boat's stern where the flames had driven them. Again, a call to Noyo brought the cutter and the mariners were saved.

The patrol boats, like their 36-foot predecessors, went out on rescue calls no matter what the weather. During the particularly fierce storms, the Noyo harbor entrance could be treacherous. One stormy night Owens and a Coast Guard officer heard that the patrol boat was in trouble. They went down to the Noyo entrance to investigate and found the cutter lying on the jetty, nearly turned over, with its side caved in. The crew had climbed off and made their own way safely to shore. The patrol boat was a total loss, and Owens recalls watching it being dismantled. A few months later a second cutter also was thrown against the jetty, although fortunately with less disastrous results.

No place on the Mendocino coast could boast fiercer storm waves than Point Cabrillo. Just two-tenths of a mile offshore the sea is 30 fathoms deep, and there is little to prevent storm waves from hitting the exposed point with full force. Harry Miller had seen waves climb the sixty-foot cliffs and sheer off a wire fence held in place by posts six inches square. But this was nothing compared to what Bill Owens was to witness.

On February 8, 1960 a storm came in from the west, beginning about 8 p.m. There was a westerly wind and the seas became increasingly rough. Soon it became apparent that conditions were going to be much worse than usual. Seas began hitting the bluff with loud and heavy force, and then started to climb the headland, actually washing across the station's flat grasslands high above the sea. The waves were now coming up the bluff, roaring across the headland, and hitting the lighthouse. The light had been turned on earlier, but the fog signal was not operating. The assistant keeper on watch called Owens to say that he could not get to the lighthouse to start the fog horns because the waves were washing past the lighthouse. Owens phoned Coast Guard headquarters in San Francisco to report that there would be no fog signal that night. The sea had become a mass of white water.

During the night the great seas increased, continuing to pound the cliffs. As Isabel Owens remembers, it sounded "like a stampede of cattle." Huge rocks were torn off the cliff face and thrown ashore by the waves. The storm continued all night and well into the next day.

As it subsided, the keepers and their families came out to inspect the damage. Rocks and gravel were everywhere. Two huge boulders, weighing close to a ton each, had been thrown ashore near the barn. Another boulder, weighing nearly two tons, had been thrown about one hundred feet beyond the edge of the bluff. When the crew entered the lighthouse, they found that the large doors at the seaward end of the fog signal room had been smashed open. A generator and an air compressor had been shoved across the room. The generator had been bolted down. On the floor there was up to a foot of gravel, sand, and rock. All of the machinery would have to be dismantled and cleaned, piece by piece. The exterior siding on the lighthouse's seaward wall had been torn off.

The waves had even gone beyond the lighthouse. A concrete walk was torn up as far as the carpenter shop and the shop's windows were broken. The area was strewn with rocks and other debris.

It would be days before the fog signal would be restored. Carpenters, electricians, and machinists all arrived to make repairs. The machinery in the fog signal room was removed, cleaned, and finally returned. A bulldozer and crew cleaned up the area, pushing rocks and boulders into the sea. Doors, windows, and siding were replaced.

After the storm, a lifetime resident of the area, a gentleman nearly ninety years old, came calling on the Owens. He wanted them to know that it was the worst storm he had ever seen along the Mendocino coast. Interestingly, there had been only a moderate wind, but great seas. During the entire storm the third order lens had operated flawlessly.

Bill Owens served at Point Cabrillo until his retirement in 1963, which marked the end of professional, civilian light keeping on the North Coast.

Coast Guardsmen continued to operate the light until the early 1970's. Then the beacon was automated. A large, reflecting beacon was mounted atop the lighthouse roof, just seaward of the tower. The fog horns were removed and a buoy with a sound signal was substituted.

Today, the entire station remains intact, from the beautiful lighthouse to the sheds. It is the best example of a complete, old-time light station in northern California. Each structure should be retained and preserved. The beach area is an abalone preserve where scientists study marine life. The old pastures are a far-flung carpet of native wild flowers.

Recently, the Coast Guard refurbished the three residences; and they are now home for some of the officers and crew (and their families) who man the 82-foot patrol boat *Point Ledge*, the current rescue boat at Noyo. It is fitting that her crew has inherited the old dwellings.

The station is currently closed to the public. It would be appropriate and very worth while if the Coast Guard would again open this historic station to visitors several hours each weekend. For the present, however, the station can be viewed from the seaward end of Heeser Drive at the northwest edge of the town of Mendocino. The lighthouse can also be seen from State Highway 1, about a mile north of the Russian Gulch Bridge. Both offer lovely views but Californians should be allowed to again visit the magnificent grounds of one of the most interesting and beautiful light stations in America.

Cutter Point Ledge *is a typical 82-foot patrol boat frequently used in Redwood Coast search-and-rescue operations. Shown leaving San Francisco Bay in 1971, this vessel is now stationed at Noyo Harbor. (U.S. Coast Guard)*

A modern 44-foot Coast Guard motor lifeboat crashes through the Redwood Coast's heavy surf. These rugged, steel lifeboats replaced the wooden 36-footers. Perhaps the finest rescue boat in the world, the "44" frequently handles rescue calls under conditions where no other type of vessel could survive. 1972. (U.S. Coast Guard)

Shelter Cove's fog bell stands at the very tip of Point Delgada. Shelter Cove can be seen in the lee of the point. 1952. (U.S. Coast Guard)

SHELTER COVE

Commercial fishermen working the coast between Noyo and Humboldt Bay commonly encounter heavy seas, high winds, strong currents and dense fog. Running for protected waters at Eureka or Fort Bragg can be a time-consuming choice, involving a considerable expenditure of fuel. But there is another alternative to "riding it out" or running; little Shelter Cove offers a fair haven in northwesterly weather. Often, when there are gale winds or thick fog at Punta Gorda and Cape Mendocino, Shelter Cove promises clear skies and calm seas.

Since the 1850's Shelter Cove has been regularly used by mariners. Before the 960-foot wharf was built in 1885, little barge-like vessels, called lighters, were towed back and forth between ship and beach using rowboats. Construction of the wharf out to deep water allowed ships to actually tie up at Shelter Cove. The port shipped tanbark (for use in tanning leather), wool, and fish. Freight and even a few tourists came ashore.

Lighthouse tender Lupine *anchored off Shelter Cove's aging wharf during construction of the fog bell station. 1936. (U.S. Coast Guard)*

In 1925 Northern California Fisheries, a combine of several West Coast fish companies, purchased the cove; and it flowered into a fishing port with a cannery, hotel, grocery store, and post office. When fishermen and ranchers were in town, Shelter Cove could boast a fair-sized community. During good years three hundred commercial fishing boats anchored in the cove at one time.

It was a beautiful place to be. The steep mountains of the King Range roll down to a grassy plateau which rims the Pacific with high cliffs. The promontory is called Point Delgada, and beneath its southern face lies Shelter Cove. There is a black-sand beach with a background of high ridges, covered with forests broken by meadows.

Despite its scenic qualities, Shelter Cove was still basically a modest cove, visited principally during the summer fishing season when the weather was good. As such, it was not to receive any navigational aid more impressive than a buoy until a very late date.

Finally, in May, 1936 the tender *Lupine* arrived, carrying a fine, old bell, cast at Mare Island Navy Yard in 1883 for the Lighthouse Service. Undoubtedly, the bell was being transferred from some light station which had been upgraded to a fog horn. The bell, machinery, and a construction crew were landed.

A wooden bell house and tower were to be erected on the eastern end of Point Delgada, overlooking the cove. Work progressed rapidly, a tall skeleton tower for the big weights and a heavily timbered gallows for the bell being the first portions completed. The bell was soon hung in the gallows. Between the bell and the tower a cement foundation was poured and the bell striking timer mounted. The timer was powered by the weights in the tower. As the weights descended, the timer's drum slowly revolved, activating a heavy, upright hammer that struck the bell every fifteen seconds. When the weights reached the bottom of the tower, an attendant would crank them back up and the ringing would continue. A small bell house was built to cover the machinery, a coat of white paint applied, and in short order the fog bell was in operation. A local resident who lived close by was hired to operate the bell during thick weather. Such a humble facility did not justify a full-time keeper.

While there had been only three major shipwrecks at Shelter Cove, a great many small craft had found themselves in distress in the area. About the same time as the bell installation, the Humboldt Bay Lifeboat Station crew was ordered to survey the cove's bottom, since the Coast Guard was giving serious consideration to establishing a rescue station there. A dory was towed down from Humboldt Bay by the 36-foot motor lifeboat; and officer-in-charge Garner Churchill and his men rowed the dory back and forth through the surf trying to determine how far down it was to bedrock. Shelter Cove never did receive a lifeboat station, although during World War II a coastal lookout was established at the cove as a part of the Beach Patrol's network.

The fog bell served for nearly a decade. To Shelter Cove fishermen there was "no sweeter sound than a bell. . . during heavy fog." The bell led many a boat to safety beneath the protective cliffs of Point Delgada.

Then, in October, 1945 the Shelter Cove fog bell was discontinued, a victim of the dissolution of the fish company. A pair of buoys henceforth served the harbor. However, the familiar bell house and tower continued to serve as a daymark. During the early 1960's the buoy tender *Magnolia* even stopped by, and its crew came ashore to give the aging structure a new coat of white paint to increase its visibility. In July, 1964, however, the gallows broke and the bell fell to the ground. That December a windstorm blew over the weight tower. Erosion was wearing the point away; and the cove's owners, Tony and Mario Machi, had to move the bell back from the edge to save it. Eventually, the Humboldt County Historical Society took possession of the bell, and it was placed on display at the College of the Redwoods, near Eureka. It is there today.

Out at Shelter Cove, Tony Machi misses the bell, a reminder of the days when he worked on a San Francisco fishing boat during the summer visits to Shelter Cove. He can still show you the hammer, some of the weights, and the timer. On the land things have changed a bit, but offshore it is much like the old days. Recently, the Pacific broke up a $175,000 commercial fishing boat that had wrecked on the rocks off the point. It makes one wonder if perhaps Shelter Cove doesn't still need the "sweet sound" of a bell.

With construction partially completed, it is possible to see (from left to right) the weights and bell tower, the bell house and timer, and the fog bell hanging in its gallows. 1936. (U.S. Coast Guard)

The weights powered the timer (at left) which every 15 seconds activated hammer (at right) to strike the fog bell. 1936. (U.S. Coast Guard)

Punta Gorda lighthouse during World War II. The small structure at left is one of the Beach Patrol's coastal lookouts. (Bureau of Land Management, Ukiah)

PUNTA GORDA LIGHTHOUSE

The loneliest stretch of California coast lies between Cape Mendocino and Shelter Cove. There are no towns fronting the sea and no harbors. Roads are few and usually rough. Throughout most of this little-known shore, travel is restricted to the hiker and the horseman. Visitors can walk the beaches and bluffs for miles and not encounter another human being. They hear only the sound of sea birds, seals, and sheep above the crash of heavy surf.

There are signs of those who came before, if one knows how to find them. Among the coarse sands and the big driftwood logs of the beaches are masts, life jackets, planks, buoys, and hulks of fishing and sailing ships. Offshore are the last monuments of lost steamers, their boilers—visible only at low tide.

This is a wild coast, a shore that collects the remains of those vessels unfortunate enough to encounter foul weather off the headland. The light keepers called its seaward arm "Windy Point," but the old Spanish mariners' term, "Punta Gorda," meaning "Massive Point," remains the favorite name of the chart makers. Both terms are accurate and descriptive. Punta Gorda itself is a high, bold cape, rounded and nearly treeless. It rises to over 800 feet in elevation, with its seaward spur, Windy Point, 140 feet high, almost hanging over the sea.

When the Lighthouse Service first considered Punta Gorda for the site of a light station, proponents could note that no less than eight ships had sunk or stranded nearby between 1899 and 1907 alone. The area was clearly a dangerous one that needed to be lighted. As early as 1890, the Lighthouse Service informed Congress that

> between Shelter Cove and Punta Gorda there are several dangerous sunken rocks off the shore that add to the hazards of navigation. In ordinary dark nights the overhanging mountains keep the shore-line in a dark shadow and confuse the best navigator as to his distance from shore, so that it is impossible to make out (Punta Gorda's) high, rounding point either from the south or from the north. Moreover, from reports made to the Coast and Geodetic Survey, it appears that little is known as to the currents of this part of the coast. The conclusion is reached, therefore, that the interests of commerce and navigation require that a light and fog-signal be established at or near Punta Gorda, California.

When the *Columbia* went down sixteen miles south of Punta Gorda in 1907, eighty-seven lives were lost. In 1908 Congress appropriated funds for the construction of the station.

Nearly a mile to the south of Punta Gorda, just below the mouth of Fourmile Creek, is a small flat. It is one of the few locations along this coast where there is enough room between the high bluffs and the sea to construct a cluster of buildings. Due to the high winds, strong currents, frequent tidal rips, and heavy seas, there could be no wharf. Materials would have to be landed by boat some distance north of the site and dragged down the sandy beach using horse-drawn sleds.

Twenty-two acres of land were purchased, giving the Government title to the narrow flat and the hills above it. Bids were let, calling for the construction of three large dwellings, a lighthouse, a fog signal building, a blacksmith-carpenter shop, an oil house, three storage sheds, sidewalks, fences, and a water and sewage system. Except for the lighthouse and fog signal, all the buildings were near-duplicates of the buildings being constructed at Point Cabrillo at this time. Probably some of the same plans were used. The position of the site required, however, that the Punta Gorda station be laid out parallel to and facing the beach, rather than at right angles to it as at Point Cabrillo.

Punta Gorda lighthouse was distinctive. It was short—just 27 feet high—but the bluff boosted its lens to an elevation of 75 feet above the

Early stages of lighthouse construction in 1910. (U.S. Coast Guard)

With its lantern room added, Punta Gorda light awaits the arrival of its lens to begin operation. C. 1911. (U.S. Coast Guard)

sea. Its concrete base was single-story and rectangular—23 feet long and 12 feet wide. It was flat-roofed and contained a watch room, drop tube, and a curving iron stairway. The concrete lower story supported an iron lantern room which held a fourth order, flashing lens. The lantern was painted black, while the concrete portion was white. The fog signal building, which looked like a schoolhouse, was equipped with an air siren. Interestingly, the siren first began its noisy task in June of 1911. The lighthouse was completed later that same year. After its lens was installed, the lamps were lighted for the first time January 15, 1912. Now, the hard part would begin.

Building Punta Gorda must have been trying, but maintaining it was maddening. Sea conditions and offshore rocks ruled out any effective supply operation by lighthouse tender. Most supplies would have to come overland, through the little town of Petrolia. There are two routes between Punta Gorda and Petrolia. One is a long, overland trail up and down high, rugged mountains. The other route is by way of the beach and the Mattole River, a distance of eleven miles. The beach route had two advantages, it was a shorter trip and—during good weather—a wagon could make the journey. It would always be the favored way to Petrolia—and civilization.

However, using even the beach route could be incredibly difficult, as Wayne Piland was to learn when he and his family arrived in the mid-1930's. During his career, Piland was to serve at three offshore lighthouses and some of the more rugged mainland stations. He rated supplying Punta Gorda as "the toughest job you ever saw."

From November through March Punta Gorda is buffeted by almost constant winds which sometimes shriek across the beach at 70 miles an hour. Heavy seas, especially in southeast weather, pound the shore, cutting off access around Windy Point. Heavy winter rains swell the Mattole River until it rages far beyond its banks. Even Fourmile Creek becomes impassable during the severest part of the season.

From the beginning, the station had a team of horses and some mules to pull the supply wagon between Punta Gorda and Petrolia. The keepers had to get their entire winter's supplies into Punta Gorda before the first of November. After that date, giant seas made it impossible to get a wagon around Windy Point. From November until the middle of May any fresh supplies were limited to what little could be carried in on horseback or by hand. Fall, then, was a time of preparation for winter. The Studebaker wagon would be piled high with cases of coffee, eight 50-pound sacks of flour, cases of corn, peas, canned soup, and the like. The wagon and its team had to be driven along the beach since there was no road. Punta Gorda's tenuous links to the outside world would be broken for long periods during the coming winter.

In between winter storms a keeper would saddle a horse and ride into Petrolia for mail and a few fresh provisions. Two gunny sacks and the saddlebag would be filled with goods from the Petrolia Cash Grocery. The wickie and his horse would then head back to the Punta before the weather worsened. It was hard going in the sand, and the horse could only be lightly loaded.

Punta Gorda's winter transportation system consisted mainly of "Old Bill." Old Bill was probably the best known horse in the 18th Lighthouse District. He had been born at a light station, served at Point Reyes, and arrived at Punta Gorda on a lighthouse tender. He was to serve there for three decades, longer than any human resident.

Old Bill had his quirks. When he approached a puddle—and there were plenty along this coast—he would try to jump it, regardless of size. This was a frightening experience for keepers more used to ships than horses. It was disastrous when he was hitched to a buggy. Most wickies preferred to walk to Petrolia, through three and one-half miles of soft sand and four and one-half miles of brushy river bottom, rather than deal with Old Bill. However, Wayne Piland and Perry Hunter, both assistant keepers, had handled horses and could cope with Old Bill. Piland got some rawhide from the carpenter shop and braided a quirt. He only used it once, and after that Old Bill was ready for the trek to Petrolia. They would leave for town as the tide was ebbing. Reaching Windy Point, Piland would sit and watch the pattern of the seas as they rushed against the big rock. He would wait for the ninth wave, usually a big, crested one, and then as the sea receded, Piland and Old Bill would gallop around Windy Point. Poor timing would mean a wet ride at best or, at worst, being swept out to sea.

Punta Gorda had a high-quality staff during the 1920's and 1930's, and it showed throughout the station. The fog signal building was a particular pride. It was probably the only fog signal building in the country that was an art gallery as well. As the Lighthouse Service had built it, the fog signal's exterior was unimpressive, but inside was a different story. There was more brasswork than almost anywhere else on the coast, and it was kept in perfect condition. There were shining brass oil cans, and shimmering measuring pitchers. There was a large brass box, designed like an old-fashioned picnic box (with double lids and a handle to place over the keeper's arm) filled with lens-cleaning materials: chamois skins, lens cloths, rouge, and whiting. Even the dust-pans were of polished brass. But most impressive of all, each wall was covered with oil paintings, primarily seascapes. They had been done by early keepers and their wives and added to the distinction of the station.

Despite having a cultural center in its fog signal building, Punta Gorda remained isolated and lonely. For a time the Lighthouse Service even considered cutting a tunnel through Windy Point to improve accessibility, but this proved impractical. Eventually, a telephone line was strung to the station, using steel beams imbedded in the rocky face of Windy Point to carry the lines around that obstacle. Winters still made it necessary for the station to be as self-sufficient as possible. Large tanks were placed both inside and outside the oil house to increase fuel storage capacity. Cows, chickens, goats, and other animals were raised. The barn's stalls and carriage space were often filled with animals and equipment. Even a hay mow was employed to supplement feed shipments.

With the arrival of World War II, the establishment of the Beach Patrol meant an increase in the number of men at Punta Gorda. Patrols from Punta Gorda operated south toward Shelter Cove. Barracks were built at the mouth of the Mattole River to guard the shore to the north.

Brand-new keepers' dwellings were spacious frame structures with pleasant, glassed-in porches. Center residence was reserved for the head keeper and his family. C. 1910. (U.S. Coast Guard)

The fog signal building at Punta Gorda came to house an art gallery as well as the twin air sirens visible on the roof. The two men to the left are keepers. (U.S. Coast Guard)

The war provided improved transportation at Punta Gorda—two new horses, Tom and Jerry, were purchased from the army in 1943. Then the war ended, the Beach Patrol was disbanded, and the light keepers and horses again had the point to themselves.

The Coast Guard now controlled the station, and there began a determined effort to improve Punta Gorda's accessibility. Tom and Jerry had proven a bit rambunctious when they overturned the station buckboard and sent two Coastguardsmen to the hospital. Old Bill, now mellowed enough so that he could be trusted to safely bring inspecting officers into the station, still could not be considered the most modern mode of transport. Building a road and providing mechanized vehicles seemed to be a logical improvement.

The Coast Guard built a road along the foot of the bluffs, from the mouth of the Mattole to Windy Point. Another section led from Windy Point to the light station. Then the station was equipped with a jeep, a scout car, and a tractor. The tractor had a large blade and pulled a sled, which could carry passengers and freight. For a time, it seemed almost as if the twentieth century had come to Punta Gorda.

Then winter came. The wind repeatedly covered much of the road with drifting sand. The seas tore at portions of the road and tossed driftwood high ashore to block other sections. The creeks and streams severed the road, washing some parts away and covering others with mud. As the season progressed, the jeep became useful only on a relatively small section of hard ground that allowed for a fairly stable, if rough, road. The scout car could be driven down the beach only when it could be gotten past Windy Point. The scout car had large, oversized tires, which when deflated would work nicely in sand; but upon reaching Lighthouse Road, it was necessary to stop and pump them back up before driving on a hard-surface road. The tractor and sleds were useful in some sections of the route, particularly since the blade was an advantage in shoving big driftwood logs off the road and removing sand dunes. None of the vehicles, however, could make the entire trip during a storm. When the rains poured, the Mattole would demolish the northern portion of the route, and Fourmile Creek would cut off the southern section. A bosun's chair had to be rigged to provide an aerial ride across Fourmile Creek during heavy rains. Eventually, a storm tossed a huge log ashore several hundred yards from the surf. It landed at just the right place and formed a natural footbridge over the creek. Perhaps it was nature condescending to help out a bit. At any rate, the Coast Guard, as had the Lighthouse Service before, saddled up Old Bill and rode into Petrolia.

By 1950, Chief Samuel "Hank" Mostovoy was officer-in-charge of Punta Gorda. Like his predecessors, Wayne Piland and Perry Hunter, Hank Mostovoy was a realist. He spent his time improving the horse

Punta Gorda's oil house was the typical concrete structure found at most light stations. (U.S. Coast Guard)

trail. Things had changed little since 1912. There were two cows, and Mostovoy and his crew made butter and cottage cheese. Wild blackberries could be gathered and served with fresh cream. There was trout in Fourmile Creek, abalone on the beach, and deer everywhere. Each fall the tractor and sled were used to bring in the winter's supply of groceries, nearly two hundred drums of fuel, and twenty tons of presto logs to burn. The station now had electricity, but the power line to the outside was so unreliable that the facility had been equipped with five generators. When Mostovoy and his men saddled the horses and pack animals to ride into Petrolia, they were often accompanied by sheep ranchers like Ed Etter. With rifles slung over their shoulders, the sheep men had the look of the Old West about them. As the keepers and ranchers rode out of the lighthouse reservation, along the dusty road in front of the rambling houses, the line of men and horses looked like it was 1880 instead of 1950.

But Punta Gorda was a costly as well as difficult station to maintain. When improved navigational equipment allowed freighters and other large vessels to operate in coastwise shipping lanes farther offshore, the Coast Guard saw the opportunity to close the station. Only commercial fishermen and occasional yachtsmen still needed Punta Gorda Light Station, and they lacked the political influence necessary to keep the station open. Hank Mostovoy would be Punta Gorda's last keeper.

In February, 1951, Punta Gorda Light Station was closed. A lighted whistle buoy was placed at the outermost rocks off the point. The lighthouse lens was removed and the sentinel reduced to a daymark. Old Bill and his fellows were sold several months later. A woman in Ferndale bought Old Bill, and he would spend his last days in the lush pastures south of Humboldt Bay.

The facility thus stood intact but abandoned. Occasional hikers and sheepherders visited the place. The three spacious dwellings still gave a genteel, turn-of-the-century feeling to the place. Their peaked, red roofs, fine brick fireplaces, and pleasant porches gave the white, two-story houses a reputation as the loveliest old homes along the southern Humboldt coast. White picket fences and wildflowers

Punta Gorda's fourth order lens was small for a coastal lighthouse. Note that the shades in the background have been pulled to protect the lens from the sun's rays. (U.S. Coast Guard)

surrounded the houses. The old fog signal building was equally picturesque. It looked much like an old, one-room country schoolhouse. However, in place of a bell on top, a rooftop platform held a pair of trumpet-like fog horns, now mute. Hikers stumbling upon the station considered it one of the surprising treasures of coastal California.

In the late 1960's, young people looking for alternative life styles began migrating from urban areas to the Redwood Coast. A few eventually moved into the old residences. They even made a real effort to clean up the area. But local reaction to the youthful newcomers was not entirely positive. A program by governmental agencies began to eliminate a number of historic, but abandoned, buildings. Bureaucrats argued that the antique frame structures had become fire hazards. Sheriff's deputies warned the young people to leave or face arrest. Once vacated, ill-advised officials decided to burn and bulldoze the buildings. In 1970 the Bureau of Land Management burned the Punta Gorda light station to the ground. Only the lighthouse and the oil house survived, since they were built of concrete.

Reaction from the public and the press held that the Redwood Coast had lost an important piece of its maritime heritage. From the first, the Bureau of Land Management officials regretted the action; and one official at the Ukiah office has said the burning was "probably a mistake."

Fortunately, the lighthouse remains today. Visitors can climb up its narrow circular stairs and pass through the little hatch into the lantern room. The old feeling of peace and solitude remains. The rich maritime past is very evident. It takes little imagination to picture keepers carrying oil up to the old vapor lamp inside the lens. Looking across the beach at the rutted road, one can readily envision "Old Bill" pulling a wagonload of supplies back from Petrolia.

One needs no imagination, however, to see the power of the sea at Punta Gorda. A huge whistling buoy, ripped from its moorings, lies on the shore below the lighthouse. At low tide the rusting boilers of two old shipwrecks can be seen. They are the bones of the passenger steamer *St. Paul*, which ran aground here in the winter of 1905, and of the *Humboldt*, an earlier wreck.

For those wishing to visit Punta Gorda, a fine map can be obtained by writing the Bureau of Land Management's District Office at 555 Leslie Street in Ukiah, California. Ask for the map of the King Range that includes the lighthouse.

The best way to reach the station is to drive from Ferndale to Petrolia. About a mile south of Petrolia turn west onto Lighthouse Road. Follow the road to the beach-front parking area. Leave your car here to hike south three and a half miles to the lighthouse. The hike is rigorous, entailing some long stretches of hiking in soft sand. However, especially in the southern half of the walk, sections of the old Coast Guard road remain intact. By carefully watching the foot of the bluffs, one can spot the good portions of the road and take advantage of its easier hiking conditions. The walk takes an hour and a half to two hours each way and should be attempted only at low tide. During this period, the surf does not come so close to Windy Point, and the wet sand is easier to walk on than dry sand. It is probably the most unspoiled piece of coastline in California. Often seals will follow hikers along the beach. Long lines of pelicans skirt the water. Beautiful native plants cling to the bluffs. From the distance, the white tower and black lantern room of the lighthouse shine in the sun. Visiting Punta Gorda light station can be a wonderful hike and picnic on a summer's day. The visitor will learn how the glorious summers made all those long winters worth while.

Pack animals return from Petrolia loaded with supplies. C. 1940. (U.S. Coast Guard)

CAPE MENDOCINO

Cape Mendocino is California's greatest headland, its westernmost point, and its most prominent coastal feature. It is a mountainous headland, the ancient landmark of the early Spanish navigators and the galleons from the Indies.

At a time when there still lived those who had spoken with Christopher Columbus, Cape Mendocino had already become important to mariners. The Spanish sailors regarded the cape as a mysterious and dangerous place, with swirling currents, heavy fog, and hidden reefs. Such a place must be the breeding ground for scurvy, so reasoned the superstitious Spanish seamen.

Those who sailed the galleons were wrong about scurvy, but they were right about the rest. Cape Mendocino is a place of strong and unpredictable currents, fierce winds, and rapidly changing weather. It is a place of great climatic change. To its north the wind blows more violently and the rain is heavier; to the south—below Punta Gorda—there is less wind and rain, but more fog. To this day the *Pacific Coast Pilot* urges that ships use "considerable caution" when approaching Cape Mendocino and warns of "numerous rocks and sunken ledges" offshore. The ocean has a heavy westerly swell that breaks not only close to shore but in deep water as well. Even the bottom of the sea contributes to the danger, for the bottom is irregular and there are frequent depth changes so that soundings may confuse the sailor as to his position. Yet nearly all coastwise vessels must pass Cape Mendocino, as it is the major turning point in the northern California shipping lanes.

The cape itself is a high, wind-blown mountain. Its rolling hills are grassy, furrowed by deep ravines in which the forest manages a foothold. The seaward face of the headland is steep, dropping almost vertically to a rocky sea. Two hundred and fifty yards offshore is beautiful Sugar Loaf, a 326-foot-high rock, dwarfed by the cape.

By the late 1860's it had become urgent that Cape Mendocino be marked by a lighthouse. On September 14, 1867, the lighthouse tender *Shubrick* was steaming up the coast with the men and materials necessary to build a light station. The *Shubrick* was in dangerous waters, and thirteen miles south of Punta Gorda she struck a rock. Water poured through a hole in the side-wheeler's hull. Fortunately, the *Shubrick* was

For nearly a century Cape Mendocino was unsurpassed in its importance to Pacific Coast shipping. Distinctively a West Coast-type beacon, it bears a striking resemblance to Point Reyes light. (U.S. Coast Guard)

just three hundred yards off Big Flat; and the tender's captain made a daring turn, running the *Shubrick* safely aground on the sandy beach. The vessel was later repaired and refloated.

While the ship was saved, the construction materials were lost. When new materials finally arrived at Cape Mendocino, everything had to be landed through the surf. Once on the beach, reaching the lighthouse site caused further difficulties. The beacon was to be built 422 feet above the sea, only part way up the bluff but high atop its most precipitous cliff. Building the beacon so high up the slopes was no ordinary task; Cape Mendocino would become the highest lighthouse site in the United States.*

Reaching the site required a long, steep climb. Mules and even a derrick were required to haul materials up the bluff. Terraces had to be dug to provide level areas for the light, dwelling, and other buildings. During summer the ground was rock-hard; but when the winter rains began, the earth became soft, mucky, and unstable. Mud slides and slip-outs occurred. Despite plans which called for a lighthouse of less than average height, the ground was too unstable to support the beacon and a large, deep hole had to be dug down to solid rock. The hole was then filled with concrete to provide a stable foundation.

The cape is one continuous slope, so steep at the site that a concrete platform had to be built around the tower's base just to provide space to walk around it. The cut in the hillside behind the tower had to be covered with stone and mortar to prevent the ridge from slumping down onto the tower.

After much effort the work was completed. The new lighthouse was a 16-sided, iron-plated, pyramidal structure with double balconies. The sentinel was 43 feet tall, painted white with a large, black lantern room. Inside, two short, semi-circular stairways led up to a beautiful first order lens. The lens would rotate very slowly, despite its many panels, since it would show a flash but once every 30 seconds.

In recognition of the cape's high winds, the entire structure was bolted to its massive concrete foundation. The finished product was the epitome of a California lighthouse—a short tower with a first order lens mounted in a large lantern room, standing atop an unusually high, windy bluff. When Point Reyes light was built a short time later, it was strikingly similar to Cape Mendocino, just as those two great headlands resemble one another both in size and weather. However, the umbrella-shaped roof at Cape Mendocino would offset it from Point Reyes and link it architecturally to such earlier beacons as Point Bonita and Farallons.

---

*The first lighthouse at Point Loma on San Diego Bay was higher. Built in 1855, it stood at 462 feet above the sea. However, in 1891 the station was relocated and a new beacon built atop cliffs only 20 feet above the sea. After 1891, therefore, Cape Mendocino was the highest lighthouse in the nation.

On December 1, 1868, Cape Mendocino was lighted. A headland used by mariners for three centuries was finally marked by great beams of light that swept nearly thirty miles out to sea.

Despite frequent thick weather, there was never to be a fog signal at Cape Mendocino. Blunts Reef is three miles to the west and the shipping lanes passed two miles beyond that.* A fog signal could not normally be heard so far offshore. Instead, a whistling buoy was moored off the reef as a sound signal.

Stations lacking fog signals were usually staffed with but one keeper. However, Cape Mendocino was to prove such a difficult station that it would always have two or—more commonly—three attendants. The wickies would be the westernmost residents of California, and they were to see hard days on the edge of the continent.

Cape Mendocino was a large station in area (the reservation comprised 171 acres, almost all of it steep, sandy and gravelly fields), but there were few buildings in the early days. Besides the lighthouse, there was a dwelling, barn, carpenter shop, and some lesser structures. More buildings would be added in coming years.

The new keepers probably had little idea of what they would face at Cape Mendocino. It would come to be considered (along with St. George Reef, Farallon Islands, Mile Rocks, Point Sur, Point Reyes, and Punta Gorda) one of the coast's roughest stations. When Cape Mendocino's keepers, in accordance with Lighthouse Service regulations, went out in the morning to raise the American flag, they found that the prevailing wind was so fierce that it was usually impossible to fly the flag. After a few mornings' attempts, the keepers probably began to have an inkling as to what lay ahead.

Trouble began during the first two winters. The lighthouse's massive concrete foundation settled unevenly and slightly cracked the tower, no small feat with a building made of thick iron plates. The new frame dwelling was more flexible as it settled, but it was less than equal to the wind. It became badly battered and began to shake apart.

In 1870 an earthquake struck and, again, the dwelling did not hold up as well as the lighthouse. The residence had to be razed and rebuilt. Three years later another earthquake hit. The ground actually split open, the crack missing the lighthouse by just fifteen feet. The crack was filled with concrete to restore stability to the site.

By 1875 the keepers were complaining of chimneys being blown down and windows shattered by the wind. The rebuilt dwelling was still no match for the gales. Eventually, it would literally be shaken apart by

---

*During the early days some vessels actually rounded Cape Mendocino using the hazardous passage inside Blunts Reef. This was such a dangerous practice that most shipping lines opposed the short cut and insurance companies refused to cover vessels using it.

the repeated windstorms. The house would become so loosened that 12-by-12-inch timber bracing would be necessary to hold it together.

In November, 1877, still another earthquake battered the reservation. However, it was the wind that frightened the keepers the most, an understandable reaction for a person who works and lives atop a 400-foot-high cliff. One night the wind was so violent that the assistant keeper fled his residence in terror, huddling in the sturdy lighthouse for safety. On many nights it was dangerous just to walk from the dwelling to the lighthouse to stand watch. A frame watch house had to be built next to the lighthouse, because trying to change watch during a windstorm could result in a wickie being blown off the cliff. The watch house was equipped with a bed to be used when the blow was a long one. Even doing indoor chores during windstorms could be hazardous. In 1880 the barn and the carpenter shop both had their windows broken by powerful gusts.

In between earthquakes and windstorms, the winter rains would soften the soil, and the buildings continued to settle. They settled so unevenly that ceilings cracked open, floors warped, and even brick walls split. Landslides and slumps continually annoyed the attendants during the wet season. In 1891 there was a particularly large landslide that left the station completely isolated. Not only did such earth movements create heavy shovel work, but they posed health hazards as well. The landslides opened the buildings to icy winds and drenching rains as well as destroying the sewage system.

Even when everything was intact, working conditions could be intolerable. The watch house lacked even a stove for heat, and the keepers often stood watch for hours in cold, wet clothes in the chill little room.

Not surprisingly, the health of the keepers and the families suffered. Throughout much of the nineteenth century, inspection reports listed the health of those serving at Cape Mendocino as "poor" or "fair." The health of the residents of most other stations during this period was described as "good" or "excellent." Several of Cape Mendocino's keepers had contracted "lung disease" and rheumatism. Conditions had become so bad that the assistant keeper and his family were forced to live in the oil house, a structure designed to accommodate kerosene, not people. By 1900 the oil house's foundation was "unsafe," the building "unsanitary" and "almost uninhabitable." The structure was listed in public documents as beyond repair. Yet it continued to be all that was provided assistant keepers. Even when a member of the assistant keeper's family died, new dwellings were still not authorized.

Throughout the nineteenth century, conditions at Cape Mendocino had been the most disgraceful on the California coast. Nature played a major role, but it seems incredible that other building projects were

Cape Mendocino's oil house was necessarily of solid rock construction. The assistant keeper and his family were forced to live here for years under the harshest conditions. The oil house stood until an earthquake destroyed it in 1923. (U.S. Coast Guard)

approved while Cape Mendocino's keepers lived without adequate shelter.

Finally, the 1906 earthquake struck San Francisco, 185 miles to the southeast. The San Andreas earthquake fault runs as far north as Cape Mendocino, and the station's chimneys were knocked down and a footbridge displaced. The 12th Lighthouse District was badly hit at many stations, and a massive rebuilding program resulted. Perhaps as a consequence, two fine new dwellings were built at Cape Mendocino in 1908.

Keeper Peter Jensen was given a two-story, three-bedroom, frame house which was quite similar to those at Punta Gorda and Point Cabrillo. Located three hundred feet southeast of the lighthouse, it was some thirty-five feet higher in elevation. The two assistants were assigned the second dwelling, a similar structure except that it was subdivided into duplex quarters with appropriate facilities for two families. It was built on another terrace, dug about one hundred feet northeast of the first keeper's dwelling and about fifty feet higher. The two residences had the distinction of being the highest light keepers' dwellings in the United States. The keeper's house had a workshop and fuel building only a few feet away, while the assistant's residence was provided with a small building which served as a workshop and tool house.

The winds prevented much ornamental landscaping, but the rich pastures were good places for animals. The wickies grazed cows for decades. Assistant P. Hunter went even further. He was a local boy, and he knew how to utilize Cape Mendocino's grasslands. The stage line ran from Ferndale to Capetown (several miles to the northeast of the lighthouse, on Bear River), and on down to Petrolia, passing along the southern edge of the lighthouse reservation. It was a difficult pull from near sea level at Bear River up over the cape and back down to sea level. Hunter raised ponies for the stage, which changed teams at the Hunter family hotel at Capetown. Coming from a Petrolia family, Hunter had access to several hundred acres of prize grassland and the knowledge to provide a nice supplement to his income as a light keeper. He continued to provide horses as long as the stage ran. When it was replaced by a gasoline vehicle, Hunter saw no future in Cape Mendocino. He then transferred to Punta Gorda to be closer to his home town and the cattle ranches to the south.

New dwelling under construction. 1908. (U.S. Coast Guard)

While in later years supplies arrived at Cape Mendocino overland from Humboldt Bay, in the early years landings had been made by lighthouse tender from the sea. Working a ship in past Blunts Reef and other dangers had proven perilous. Passing through the surf was even more hazardous. In 1881 a tender (either the old *Shubrick* or the recently arrived *Manzanita*) anchored just outside the breakers, probably off the beach that is just to the south of the cape. Lighthouse Inspector McDougal was to make the quarterly inspection, and he was put over the side in a small boat. Commander McDougal began rowing ashore, the light keepers undoubtedly waiting on the beach to help pull the boat ashore. As the inspector attempted to pass through the surf, the breakers became unmanageable. The boat capsized and Commander McDougal was drowned. According to tradition, he was dragged down by the heavy bag of gold coins fastened to his waist, since he was bringing the keepers their pay. (A year later, McDougal's widow, Kate, was appointed keeper of Mare Island lighthouse at Vallejo, a position she would hold for thirty-five years.)

The Cape Mendocino area would be the scene of at least nine major shipwrecks, a number kept relatively small by the combined efforts of Cape Mendocino light and the *Blunts Reef Lightship*, placed off the reef in 1905. When the passenger steamer *Bear* ran ashore at Bear River in 1916, survivors at first attempted to come ashore through the heavy surf. The lifeboats were capsized, and five persons drowned. After witnessing what Cape Mendocino's breakers had done to their pulling boats, those still aboard the *Bear* manned the remaining lifeboats and rowed out to sea—to the *Blunts Reef Lightship* and safety. Much worse was the wreck of the liner *Alaska*, which struck Blunts Reef in 1921. Forty-two lives were lost; and when the crew of the Humboldt Bay Lifeboat Station arrived, they found only the *Alaska's* mast sticking above the water.

In 1924, M. M. Palmer became a keeper at Cape Mendocino. Palmer was well aware of the area's recent shipwrecks, and he kept a sharp eye on the sea. One day in October, 1926, Palmer saw that a passing steam schooner, the *Everett*, was afire. A telephone line had been built, its wires placed underground in some locations for protection from the high winds, and Palmer quickly sent out a call for assistance. The situation was very serious. After the fire had started, the *Everett's* crew had been gassed by fumes. Palmer's alertness allowed a ship to arrive in time to rescue the helpless crew, and he was credited with saving their lives.

Through the 1930's Palmer worked with first assistant P. Rickard, and together they ran a well-managed light station. The dwellings were still lighted by kerosene and heated by burning presto logs in the brick fireplaces. With adequate shelter, Cape Mendocino could be a wonderful and beautiful place, especially during spring when the wildflowers

bloomed in the grasslands. Sea lions barked from the beach below, and the gentle sound of the wind could be heard as it flowed around Sugar Loaf. The light-blue sea could be seen stretching far beyond the little red lightship off the reef.

At the outbreak of World War II, a coastal lookout was established near the lighthouse. Cape Mendocino's amazing view was to prove its worth in short order. On December 20, 1941, the tanker *Emidio* was torpedoed twenty miles off Blunts Reef by a Japanese submarine. Cape Mendocino's lookout, Coastguardsman Walter G. Muenther, was immediately informed of the incident and his were the eyes which watched over other American vessels as they rounded the headland that frightening afternoon.

After the war, the station continued to be manned. Then, in 1950, the Coast Guard began the long road to automation on the Redwood Coast. Punta Gorda was the first to lose its keepers; and a few days later—on March 3, 1951—Cape Mendocino Light Station was unmanned and converted to automatic operation.

The first order lens was removed, to be displayed at the Humboldt County Fairgrounds in Ferndale. The old lens was placed in a wooden information center and ticket booth which somewhat resembles the actual lighthouse. It remains there today, and can be seen even when the fair is not in session.

A pair of modern, rotating airways beacons (which had their own small prisms) were installed in the Cape Mendocino lighthouse lantern room, and the antique sentinel continued its time-honored duty. Eventually, however, even the rotating beacons were removed; and today the lighthouse is dark.

A light still shines from the cape, but it emanates from a double-drum, reflecting airways beacon atop a steel pole, 515 feet above the surf. It is maintained by electricians from the Humboldt Bay Coast Guard Station who arrive once or twice a month to service the light, a radio beacon antenna, and a small structure filled with electrical generating and radio beacon equipment.

All of the interesting wooden structures are gone now. In 1960 the Coast Guard burned the frame buildings in response to "squatters." No consideration was given to historical significance, and the dwellings were destroyed completely.

Fortunately, the lighthouse was spared and it stands today. The old sentinel still serves as a daymark for commercial fishermen and small craft, a valuable feature since mariners have historically confused Cape Mendocino with False Cape, four and a half miles to the north. The

Companion navigational aid to Cape Mendocino light station was the Blunts Reef lightship. Storm warnings fly from Number 100's foremast while the great rolling hills of the cape loom in the distance. 1952. (U.S. Coast Guard)

consequences of such an error have led to several major shipwrecks.

Presently, the lighthouse is closed to the public. There is a genuine need to reopen the lighthouse so that citizens can return to visit such an historic site. Cape Mendocino is a maritime landmark dating from the days of the Spanish galleons, the former home of light keepers who were the westernmost residents of California. Cape Mendocino is the great turning point of the Pacific Coast shipping lanes, and its light was for over a century perhaps the most important in California. From early spring until late fall, the cape is usually blessed with good weather and almost magical scenery. The old sentinel and the terraces of the former dwellings lend themselves to a fine small park. Visitors would see one of the earliest and best examples of a Pacific Coast lighthouse, a sentinel unquestionably worthy of being included in the National Register of Historic Places.

At this time, visitors must view the beacon from a distance. The trip from Ferndale to Petrolia is pastoral and unspoiled. When the road finally reaches the sea, the visitor is at Cape Mendocino. The road descends the massive bluff which is the cape, and the high rock just offshore to the north is Sugar Loaf. Drive south along the beach a half mile or more and look back to see the upper portion of the lighthouse. Above it, the automatic airways beacon flashes day and night. Here is the farthest west and most exposed of all California's headlands.

Scenic, 326-foot-high Sugar Loaf rock has long been associated in sailors' memories with Cape Mendocino light. New, automatic lights can be seen in the sentinel's lantern room, but the "umbrella-shaped" roof places Cape Mendocino architecturally among the earliest Pacific Coast lighthouses built in the 1850's and 1860's. (U.S. Coast Guard)

SAN FRANCISCO AND BLUNTS REEF LIGHTSHIPS

There are locations where a major navigational aid is required but where erecting a lighthouse would be impossible. California has two such places. Both locales are on busy shipping lanes where the water is over one hundred feet deep, yet nearby there are grave navigational hazards too far offshore to be marked by a lighthouse. At such places, the Lighthouse Service moored a vessel which served as a floating lighthouse. Called a lightship, these vessels rode at anchor for months at a time in all kinds of weather, marking a channel and warning of hidden dangers. As is true of lighthouses, lightships displayed a light, sounded a fog signal, and—in later years—emitted a radio beacon signal. The hulls of these vessels were generally bright red with the name of their station painted in huge white letters on both sides of the hull.

Despite the incredible length of the Pacific Coast, less than ten per cent of America's lightship stations were located here. Even after the last Pacific Coast light vessel station was established in 1909, the west could boast but five stations while the Atlantic Coast and the Great Lakes could claim a total of forty-six lightships in position.

The discrepancy resulted primarily from the differing geography of the two regions. Generally, the Pacific Coast is a shoreline where deep water suddenly encounters high cliffs. Such conditions are ideal for lighthouse construction, rendering light vessels unnecessary. In contrast, the land and the water of the Atlantic Coast and the Great Lakes blend gradually. There are numerous shoals, banks, and ledges. Some of these are too deep to allow for lighthouse construction, but shallow enough to represent a hazard to mariners, especially during heavy weather.

Nevertheless, there were places on the West Coast where lightships had to be established. Canada had only one Pacific Coast lightship station, but it was the first to be established on the West Coast. The *Fraser River Lightship* was first moored off British Columbia in 1866. This vessel was eventually discontinued, but in 1905 the *Sand Heads Lightship* was placed on station to mark the same area.

America's first Pacific Coast lightship was built in San Francisco by the Union Iron Works in 1892. Assigned the number 50, this 123-foot-long, wooden sailing vessel became the *Columbia River Lightship*, serving just outside the river's bar from 1892 until a more modern ship replaced her in 1909.

San Francisco Lightship, Number 70, *was California's first light vessel. Note the twin fog whistles just forward of her stack and the oil lanterns hanging from her masts. (U.S. Coast Guard)*

San Francisco could claim the distinction of having produced the first American lightship on the West Coast as well as the distinction of having the first California lightship stationed there. The San Francisco bar is a large and dangerous place. It forms a great semi-circle stretching from Point Bonita on the north to the southern limits of San Francisco's shore. In smooth weather many parts of the bar can be crossed with safety, but during heavy seas the area becomes a mass of huge breakers. On such days, the bar's extent can be clearly seen from shore. The Lighthouse Service determined that a light vessel must be placed to mark the main shipping channel leading into San Francisco Bay. The lightship would guide ships across the bar at its safest and deepest part, helping them to avoid dangerous Potato Patch Shoal off Point Bonita.

The first San Francisco lightship, *Number 70*, was quite an improvement over earlier lightships. Built of steel, she was a self-propelling steam vessel in an era when most lightships were unpowered and built of wood. Her coal-fired boilers not only supplied steam for a 12-inch fog whistle (the largest-size whistle in use in California), but helped

America's first Pacific Coast lightship, old Number 50, *shown after she was blown off station in 1899 while serving at the Columbia River bar. Driven high ashore, she had to be hauled through the woods to be launched. (U.S. Lighthouse Service photograph)*

power generators which fed electricity to her lights. Electrical lighting was *Number 70*'s ultra-modern feature.

Built in Portland, Oregon, *Number 70* arrived in San Francisco on March 11, 1898, tying up at the Yerba Buena Island Lighthouse Depot. Four days later her crew was complete, and by the 21st of March a trial run inside the Bay proved satisfactory. On April 3, the vessel was taken to the Lighthouse Service's Pier 15 in San Francisco to have her bunkers filled with coal. Fresh water and a goodly store of food and supplies was put on board.

Then, on April 7, 1898, accompanied by the tender *Madroño, Number 70* steamed out the Golden Gate. Using distant Alcatraz and Fort Point lighthouses as range lights to determine her exact location, *Number 70* dropped anchor three miles outside the bar in 108 feet of water. That evening both her light and fog signal began operation and California had its first lightship. With her light flashing and her whistle blasting, she was an effective guidepost for ships seeking San Francisco Bay.

A lightship's job is never easy. Pitching and rolling at the end of a chain, she must stay moored where no other ship would ever drop anchor. During storms, she is required to remain on station when all other ships can run for safety. Thus, it was no surprise when on May 14, 1899, during a severe northwest gale, the *San Francisco Lightship* broke adrift from her moorings. With large and increasing seas, the small auxiliary anchor was no match for the Pacific. There was no alternative but to haul in the broken anchor chain and steam back to Yerba Buena Island Depot for new moorings. It was 39 hours before the ship could return, and during that time the bar's outer reaches were completely unmarked. It would not be the last time the Pacific was too much for the ship.

Communications were not much better than the weather. To be sure, the little gasoline schooner *Ida A.* came alongside once every two weeks bringing mail, supplies and sometimes relief crewmen. Communications with shore, though, were still limited to hailing an inbound vessel or sending carrier pigeons to shore with messages. Both systems needed to be improved.

In 1899, a rather interesting alliance of the Lighthouse Service, the press and a group of scientists centered their interest on the *San Francisco Lightship*. All three groups were striving for instant communication, the Lighthouse Service's interest stemming from numerous tragedies at its far-flung, isolated stations which might have been avoided (or at least alleviated) through improved communication. The press's interest, of course, lay in achieving a faster means of relaying news to the public. The scientists had been stimulated by Guglielmo Marconi's astounding transmission of wireless messages from a British lightship to shore.

Relief Number 76 *spent her entire 56-year career as a relief vessel on the Pacific Coast. 1933. (U.S. Coast Guard)*

On August 19, 1899, the tug *Reliance* brought technicians and equipment out to the *San Francisco Lightship.* Wireless telegraphic equipment was installed in *Number 70's* engine room and wire was strung from her masts. The lightship's electrical generators made her ideally suited to the experiment at hand. Transmissions attempted on land had failed, and now an attempt would be made to send a radio message over the water from the light vessel to a station set up at the Cliff House in San Francisco.

The San Francisco *Call,* a local newspaper, was underwriting the costs. The Army transport ship *Sherman* was expected to return soon with California's contingent of troops from the Spanish-American War. The *Sherman's* arrival was the great event of the season and should the *Call* learn of its arrival first, it would have the newspaper scoop of the year.

Sure enough, on August 23, 1899, at 5:15 p.m., the *Sherman* came close by the lightship in-bound for San Francisco with the California volunteers on board. The *Sherman* was early and only a single electrician, a Mr. Fisher, was on board *Number 70.* He had been running the dynamo all day practicing sending, and he was still not sure the apparatus worked. With the *Sherman*'s arrival, Fisher had no choice but to immediately send his message and hope that it was heard. He began pounding out the message: "SHERMAN IS SIGHTED, SHERMAN IS SIGHTED," over and over.

The lightship transmission was, indeed, received in San Francisco. As a result, it was possible to arrange for a huge parade along San Francisco's Market Street at a definite time. The troops paraded through the heart of the City as packed crowds, alerted by the wireless message (and the *Call*) cheered them on.

Although the crowds were pleased by the return of the soldiers, it was the wireless message itself that was most significant. The *Lighthouse Bulletin* proudly recorded: "this was the first wireless message to be sent not only from a lightship in this country, but from any point in the United States." The *Bulletin* pointed out that the San Francisco transmission occurred three months before any other wireless telegraph installation on an American ship. The *San Francisco Lightship* had been on station barely a year and she had already made history.

Radio communication, however, was still in its infancy, and the wireless was soon removed from the lightship. Eventually, the modern electric lights were discontinued as well. Keeping the electrical generators going required 266 tons of coal annually, six times the amount her steam fog whistle required in some years. Conventional oil lamps proved to be a more economical substitute. *Number 70* had met the twentieth century and found that it did not work very well.

The eternal problems of the sea remained, however. In February, 1902, a "fierce southern gale" arose, parting *Number 70*'s moorings and forcing her to run for port. Even after repairs were made at Yerba Buena Island, the bar was still so rough that the lightship could not return to her position for many hours.

Just staying on station in reasonably fair weather could be dangerous. On February 9, 1903, the schooner *Novelty*, carried along by a strong Golden Gate tide, collided with the lightship. On May 28, 1910, the four-masted schooner *Cecilia Sudden* rammed *Number 70*, "inflicting heavy damage to the upper parts of the light-vessel."

Even when she was moored in San Francisco Bay, *Number 70* had her problems. As luck would have it, the ship was in the city for repairs when the 1906 earthquake struck. The *San Francisco Lightship* had to flee to Yerba Buena Island Depot to prevent being burned by the ensuing fire. The Depot would seem a safe enough place, but in 1915 the Navy launch *Castro* ran into *Number 70* while she was moored there.

The *San Francisco Lightship* was often buried in heavy fog. In 1915 she reported 2,145 hours of fog for the year, probably more than any light vessel in the country. The next year it was worse—there was a total

Blunts Reef was one of the roughest lightship stations in America. Number 83, first vessel to serve here, pitches upward, straining against her anchor chain. C. 1920's. (U.S. Coast Guard)

Blunts Reef, Number 100 *pitches in heavy seas. (U.S. Coast Guard)*

of 2,221 hours of fog. For an incredible 25 per cent of the year, the *San Francisco Lightship* was fog-bound! During those dark, endless days, *Number 70*'s fog whistle gave an ear-shattering, two-second blast every 13 seconds. The number of whistle blasts her crew endured in the span of a year staggers the imagination.

Whatever else one could say about her, *Number 70* had proven that lightships were valuable aids to mariners on the California coast. By 1898 the Coast and Geodetic Survey, the Revenue Cutter Service, and the Lighthouse Service had all become convinced that a lightship was also needed 185 miles to the north at Blunts Reef off Cape Mendocino.

In retrospect, the very idea of placing a light vessel off Cape Mendocino seems a bit audacious. The Lighthouse Service already had trouble enough preventing the cape's seasonal high winds from blowing its light station to pieces and carrying the keepers away. It seems almost incredible that the Service would attempt to moor a small ship year round at such a location.

Blunts Reef itself consists of only two small, black rocks awash at high tide; but in actuality it is merely the outermost of countless rocks scattered for nearly three miles off Cape Mendocino and for four miles both north and south. Commissioner of Lighthouses George R. Putnam called Blunts Reef "a wild and desolate section of California coast."

The Lighthouse Service realized that only a lightship could adequately mark the busy coastwise shipping lanes off the Cape: "The light shown at Cape Mendocino (lighthouse) is sufficient on clear nights, but in thick weather it is of little, if any, use, and the light station here is without a fog signal." There was no fog signal at Cape Mendocino light because the shipping lanes ran outside Blunts Reef, too distant for a land-based fog signal to be reliably audible.

A modern, first-class, steel lightship powered by steam would have the best chance of surviving off Blunts Reef. Thus, in March, 1903, Congress approved $90,000 to build lightship *Number 83*. The 112-foot-long vessel was built in Camden, New Jersey, equipped with three oil lights on both her masts and featured a steam fog whistle 12 inches in diameter. The Lighthouse Service was particularly proud of the new vessel's crew quarters. Described as "staterooms," the living quarters were "roomy, comfortable, and well ventilated," quite a contrast to many of the Service's other ships.

In company with *Relief Lightship, Number 76*, the *Blunts Reef Lightship, Number 83*, arrived in San Francisco on June 4, 1905, after a "successful voyage of 110 days from New York." After receiving fresh supplies, *Number 83* steamed off for Blunts Reef. On June 28, 1905, she took her station and California had its second lightship.

While the *San Francisco Lightship* was anchored at the foggiest lightship station on the West Coast and probably in the entire nation, the *Blunts Reef Lightship*'s station was to prove to be perhaps the roughest on either coast.

The storms at Blunts Reef were incredible. In one eight-month period, the lightship was blown off station by terrible storms on six occasions!*As if the storms were not enough, on January 2, 1910, the steam schooner *Del Norte*, bound from Crescent City to San Francisco, rammed *Number 83* with such heavy damage that the lightship had to be rushed to San Francisco for repairs.

On April 27, 1912, *Number 83* managed a revenge of sorts for all those rammings that lightships had been receiving. Leaving the wharf at Pier 15 in San Francisco, she rammed not one, but two, merchant ships, the *Newberg* and the *Manuka*.

Back on station, one foggy June night in 1916 at 1:30 a.m., the lookout on the *Blunts Reef* heard a lifeboat hailing the light vessel. The passenger steamer *Bear* had fatally stranded north of Cape Mendocino, and lifeboats full of survivors began pulling alongside *Number 83*. Before the night was over, nine lifeboats, guided by *Number 83*'s fog whistle, had arrived at the lightship and one hundred fifty-five survivors were taken on board. With a heavy surf and dense fog, the lightship had proven a safer haven than trying to pass through the breakers to shore. The lightship crew's ability to be adequate hosts was severely limited, although the survivors were provided with hot coffee and blankets. The following morning the steamer *Grace Dollar* responded to pleas for assistance and arrived to take the survivors on board.

During this first quarter of the twentieth century, all of America's West Coast light vessels had been equipped with a special type of sound signal. Called a "submarine bell," this device consisted of a bell suspended from the bottom of a lightship at a depth of twenty-five to thirty feet in the water. Operated by compressed air, the bells were installed when the Lighthouse Service discovered that sound traveled more effectively through water than through air. A conventional surface fog signal (such as a compressed air horn) could, at best, be heard five or six miles at sea. Under ideal conditions, submarine bells were reported at distances of fifteen and more miles.

Old *Number 70* clanged out seven strokes followed by four seconds of silence as its signal. Out on Blunts Reef, *Number 83*'s submarine bell struck eight strokes, was silent for three seconds, and then followed with three more strokes, providing its signal of "83." The three light vessels in the Pacific Northwest likewise struck their numbers.

The efficiency of submarine bells required that all ships be equipped with suitable receiving equipment attached to their hull on the bow and telephonically connected to the bridge. Unfortunately,

---

*On the following dates: November 3, 1906; December 9, 1906; January 6, 1907; February 24, 1907; March 22, 1907, and June 19, 1907.

many ships did not have the necessary apparatus and eventually sub-marine bells joined the ranks of other extinct beasts.

Number 70 off San Francisco's bar and *Number 83* on Blunts Reef necessarily returned to port occasionally for repairs. In the earliest days, when *Number 70* was the state's only lightship, a buoy with a gas light took her place or—less commonly—the tender *Madroño* was moored off the bar as a makeshift light vessel. Neither system worked very well, so when *Blunts Reef Lightship* had arrived in 1905, *Number 76* had come with her. Built at Staten Island, New York, the 117-foot-long vessel had the usual oil lights and fog whistle. *Number 76's* role would be to serve as the sole *Relief Lightship* for the entire West Coast.

Besides San Francisco and Blunts Reef, there were lightships stationed off the Columbia River bar and (since 1898) at Umatilla Reef, Washington. A fifth, and final, lightship station was established at Swiftsure Bank, Washington, in 1909 to mark the entrance to Puget Sound.

No region in America needed a relief lightship more than did the Pacific Coast. When *Number 76* arrived, the *Columbia River Lightship* (old *Number 50*) had been blown ashore. The *Umatilla Reef* light vessel had been transferred to the Columbia River bar, leaving Washington State's worst hazard to navigation unmarked. Consequently, *Number 76* began her life-long career as a "stand-in" at Umatilla Reef on June 17, 1905.

The following year found the *Relief* on station at San Francisco while *Number 70* was in port. *Number 76* was immediately subjected to the same perils that befell the regular light vessel: a barkentine rammed her and the fierce winds blew her off station.

The year 1909 was a significant one for relief light vessels. Old *Number 50*, pioneer West Coast lightship, was retired from Columbia River station. She was sent to Yerba Buena Island and, for a short time, served as a relief light vessel in California. Then the aging vessel was decommissioned and sold to private interests.

Number 50's retirement was made possible by the arrival, in January, 1909, of the "Lightship Flotilla," a fleet of three light vessels and three lighthouse tenders sent west by the Lighthouse Service to upgrade navigational aids on the Pacific Coast. Among the six vessels, only the tender *Sequoia* made San Francisco her permanent home port, the other five departing for the Pacific Northwest or Hawaii. The new ships did, however, make it possible for *Number 76* to become full-time relief vessel for California's two stations.

The 1920's saw little change. The same ships continued flashing their lights and blowing their fog signals, with annual relief periods when *Number 76* took their stations while they returned to port.

By now the Lighthouse Service had learned a great deal about light-

ship design. Since the turn of the century, many improvements had been made in lightship design. Anchors and chain had been improved, lessening the chance of being swept away during storms. To diminish rolling, bilge keels were placed below the waterline along the ships' sides. Both the height of bow and the "sheer" (the height of the bow in relation to the height of the stern) were increased so that the decks kept drier. The metacentric height of lightships was reduced so that the vessels would "sit" in the water more sturdily. Hawse-pipes (the opening where the anchor chain passes out of the ship) were placed literally on the bow instead of the usual position slightly aft of the bow, helping keep the lightship headed directly into the current. Wood construction was replaced by steel, and unpowered vessels were retired in favor of propeller-driven steamships. Lightship quarters became more spacious, and radios were installed for instant communication. The safety and comfort of the crew was greatly improved, along with the lightship's "sea-keeping ability"—that is, her ability to stay on station in any kind of weather.

Then, in 1930, the first of six new diesel-electric lightships was built. By substituting diesel-electric power for steam, the new lightship, *Number 100*, could get under way within five minutes, a tremendous improvement over the older steam vessels. When a mooring broke, or if the anchor dragged and the lightship were blown off-station, having almost instant power would be a huge advantage. Substitution of diesel-electric for steam equipment also resulted in a reduction of about one hundred tons of displacement. This meant that the new vessels offered less resistance to the sea and, consequently, ship and crew took less of a beating. On *Number 100* diaphone air horns replaced the old steam whistles and reliable electric lights were installed throughout the ship. A 7,000-pound mushroom anchor and 900 feet of heavy chain gave assurance that she would not be easily forced off station.

As the new lightships were completed, most were sent to the roughest stations in the nation, including Nantucket Shoals (furthest offshore lightship in the world), Frying Pan Shoals (south of dread Cape Hatteras), and Swiftsure Bank (off Vancouver Island's stormy western shore).

The very first of all these vessels, *Number 100*, was sent to perhaps the roughest station of all—Blunts Reef.

When *Number 100* first took up her station at Blunts Reef on February 10, 1930, the 133-foot-long vessel was—according to maritime historian James Gibbs—"probably the finest lightship in the United

Blunts Reef Lightship, Number 100 *had just been completed when this picture was taken. Probably the finest lightship in the world at that time, her mushroom anchors and bilge keel are clearly visible. C. 1929. (U.S. Coast Guard)*

States and equal to any in the world." Her fifth order lantern would light Blunts Reef for the coming 30 years.

The days of the oldest lightships were now coming to a close. When *Number 100* arrived at her new post, the original *Blunts Reef Lightship, Number 83*, was transferred to the San Francisco bar. The pioneer San Francisco lightship, *Number 70*, was then retired. Rechristened the *Tondelayo, Number 70* saw private service in Alaska, reportedly being lost in Clarence Strait about 1941. *Columbia River*, later *Relief Number 50*—decommissioned as a lightship in 1909—was still afloat working for San Francisco's Red Salmon Canning Company, but after 1935 she was beached near Antioch on Suisun Bay.

Relief Number 76 continued to relieve California's light vessels, but she was rebuilt, lengthened to 129 feet, her bow redesigned, and equipped with an electrically lighted lens lantern. *Number 83*, now the *San Francisco Lightship*, was similarly modernized.

The 1930's was the last decade of Lighthouse Service operation. The tenders *Sequoia* and *Lupine* still steamed out to the lightships, bringing supplies, mail, and relief crewmen. Standard practice was to tie the tender to the already moored lightship's stern, letting the drift of the current keep the tender safely astern of the light vessel. Pulling boats were then rowed between the two ships, transferring personnel and provisions. At the end of the decade, in 1939, the Lighthouse Service was taken under the control of the Coast Guard.*

Lightships were a boon to shipping the world over, and after December, 1941, those using the California light vessels included enemy submarines. Japanese and German submarine officers often would lay off lightships to torpedo freighters and tankers as they passed by. During both world wars, this was especially common in Europe, but it occurred off the American East Coast as well. After Pearl Harbor, both the *Columbia River* and *Blunts Reef* lightships were used as guide posts by Japanese submarines. Taking its position off the *Columbia River Lightship*, an enemy submarine attempted to shell Oregon's Fort Stevens. Fortunately, at the onset of hostilities the lightship had been secretly remoored one mile south of its charted position. The shells fell harmlessly in the woods, exactly one mile south of the fort.

At Blunts Reef, the results were not so fortunate. The tanker *Emidio* was sunk, its surviving crewmen finding refuge aboard *Blunts Reef, Number 100*.

In 1950 the first Coast Guard-designed lightships were built. One of the first of these, *WLV 612*, was sent to replace *Number 83* on the San Francisco bar. Arriving on station in 1951, this steel, diesel-powered,

*The Coast Guard renumbered all the lightships. *Number 76* became *Number 504; Number 86* became *Number 508; Number 100* became *Number 523.* The Coast Guard used the letters WAL, and later WLV to denote a lightship. However, for the sake of clarity, we will refer to all the early ships using their original numbers.

At least once a year, all of California's lightships returned to the Lighthouse Depot on San Francisco Bay's Yerba Buena Island. Note the buoys in for repair. Number 100 *during the 1930's. (U.S. Coast Guard)*

128-foot-long ship boasted a top speed of 11 knots and a crew of 16 to 18 men. To guard against floating objects ramming her, a six-foot-wide, steel band was built into her sides, three feet above the waterline and three feet below it.

Old *Number 83*, the original Blunts Reef vessel, was dispatched to become a relief lightship in the Pacific Northwest. She had seen 46 years of duty on the California coast.

When the new *San Francisco Lightship, WLV 612*, returned to port for maintenance, her place was taken by aging *Relief, Number 76*. By 1954, she was fifty years old, still spending half the year bobbing up and down on station. Serving such a fog-bound coast on *Number 76* was particularly hard on the ship's commanding officer. The *Relief's* foremast was hollow, serving as an air chamber for the compressed air fog horns. With each blast, the air chamber refilled. Unfortunately, the captain's cabin was placed almost directly under the fog horns with the air chamber running about two feet from the skipper's bunk. During foggy weather, the *Relief's* master moved out of his cabin and in with the crew.

Number 76 lasted until 1960, when another modern Coast Guard light vessel, *WLV 605*, was transferred to Blunts Reef, after serving as the *Overfalls Lightship* off the New Jersey coast. A sister ship of *WLV 612*, the new vessel made it possible for the Coast Guard to decommission the 56-year-old *Relief*. At last report, *Number 76* rests abandoned along a Seattle waterway.

There were now three lightships on duty in California. They would be the last of their breed to light the Golden State's coast.

From 1960 to 1969 *WLV 605* remained off Blunts Reef. During this same period the beautiful *Number 100* was designated the *Relief*. *WLV 612* remained on duty at the San Francisco bar. In 1969 the ships were rotated a final time. The last *Blunts Reef Lightship* would be *WLV 612;* the final *San Francisco Lightship* was *Number 100*, and the West Coast's last *Relief* vessel was *WLV 604*.

During these final years, buoy tenders, such as the *Magnolia*, supplied the *San Francisco Lightship* from Yerba Buena Island. The *Blunts Reef* was served by the cutter *Avoyel* from Fields Landing on Humboldt Bay or by small motor lifeboats from the Humboldt Bay Lifeboat Station.

The last years of lightship operation were as wild and dangerous as they had been during the first decades of the century. The fear of being

The 375-millimeter lens lantern came to be the standard lens on California light-ships by the 1930's. Number 100. (U.S. Coast Guard)

Shown here on station off the Columbia River bar, Relief WLV 604 *was the last West Coast relief vessel. Her twin, vertical mushroom trumpet fog horns can be seen just aft of the flying bridge. 1971. (U.S. Coast Guard)*

The Coast Guard built Blunts Reef WLV 612, *last lightship to serve at that isolated station. 1971. (U.S. Coast Guard)*

rammed had probably increased as freighters, tankers, and military ships became much larger. These vessels used the lightships as a "target" in the sense that they steered toward the lightship when entering a channel. Mariners were expected to correct their course so that they passed nearby, but not dangerously close. Not all of them made such corrections.

On the Atlantic Coast and in Europe a number of lightships had been rammed, sending some of them to the bottom along with their crews. Northern California's heavy fog caused ramming to be a regular occurrence during the early years. The fear still haunted lightship crews, but several protective maneuvers could now be taken.

When a vessel came too close the lightship could begin blowing her horn as a danger signal. Simultaneously, the crew would begin letting out their anchor chain, so as to drift off station and out of the way. The doors of air-tight compartments (standard on modern lightships) could be secured. Finally, the light vessel's radio beacon would be immediately shut off, since the on-coming vessel would be using it as a homing device. The sudden termination of the radio beacon signal would, hopefully, cause the navigator to question his position and alter his collision course. Still, the hazard of being rammed remained.

Neither did improved moorings mean that a modern ship could no longer be blown off station. *Relief WLV 605* carried a 9,600-pound mushroom anchor attached to a heavy-duty chain thirteen shots long. In calm weather, the *Relief* rode with seven to nine shots out. As the severity of conditions increased, more shots were let out. This provided more holding weight as additional chain lay on the bottom. It also minimized the likelihood of the chain becoming taut and dragging the anchor along the bottom or breaking a link. Consequently, in heavy weather the *Relief* rode with up to twelve (of her thirteen) shots out. It was a lot of chain to help hold a ship barely over one hundred feet long in position. The crew of the *San Francisco Lightship, Number 100*, found that any time the wind exceeded 35 knots, her engines also must be started to help her maintain position and keep from dragging anchor.

Twice during 1969-71, *Relief WLV 605* was blown off position. One occurrence was off the Columbia River bar when heavy seas and 60-knot-per-hour winds blew the ship off station. The other incident was at Blunts Reef when winds reached 70 to 80 knots and the seas 15 to 20 feet in height. The *Relief's* radar was destroyed and the ship spent the night being battered about, uncertain of her position. The big cutter *Resolute* was dispatched from San Francisco to assist, but by morning the storm diminished and the lightship was safely remoored.

Removing sick crewmen was another acute problem during heavy weather. A fireman aboard the *Blunts Reef WLV 612* suffered a heart attack during a winter storm. Humboldt Bay Coast Guard Station's

44-foot motor lifeboat succeeded in reaching the lightship and bringing the man safely on board; but while returning across the Humboldt Bay bar huge waves shattered the "44"'s windshield, severely lacerating the faces of the crew.

Loneliness and confinement were as bad as the weather. In the earliest days, Lighthouse Service personnel had to scour San Francisco's waterfront to round up a crew. It was an unpleasant task, because the lighthouse officials had to compete with "crimps" who still shanghaied unsuspecting sailors. Later, the Lighthouse Service ran afoul of the maritime unions over wages and working conditions. The San Francisco waterfront was a turbulent and sometimes violent place; and shipping on a Lighthouse Service vessel was often viewed as a dangerous and underpaid berth. Recruiting crews to serve on tenders and light vessels was often difficult.

The Coast Guard, using enlisted men, had less of a problem staffing its ships, but its crews still experienced the old strains. The *San Francisco Lightship*'s enlisted men found it painful to watch pleasure boats pass by filled with young couples enjoying an outing. "Channel fever," growing anxiety as liberty day approached, bothered some of the crew. On Blunts Reef there were not even any people to wave at.

Long watches, sometimes sixteen hours a day, helped pass the time. Daily jobs included maintaining a live watch on the light, fog signal, and radio beacon to assure that they were sending their proper signals. These duties were particularly important aboard a relief lightship, because the signals varied with each station. Besides constant preventative maintenance, crewmen cared for the ship's diesel engines, electric motors, boilers, pumps, electronic gear, radio equipment, and the like. Along with daily food preparation, cooks were responsible for bringing proper food on board and carefully storing it. A boatswain's mate directed the deck crew.

Early in 1971, the Coast Guard announced that the era of California's lightships would come to a close and the vessels would permanently leave their stations. For many years the Coast Guard had been experimenting with various methods of replacing its light vessels, which were costly and difficult to maintain. By 1967 it had developed "large navigational buoys," 40 feet in diameter and 42 feet high, which automatically operated a light, fog signal, and radio beacon. Painted in lightship colors, they also made satisfactory day marks. By replacing lightships with these "super buoys," the Coast Guard could annually save many thousands of dollars. In July, 1967, New York's *Scotland Lightship* became the first vessel to be replaced by a large navigational buoy. It was not the last.

On April 26, 1971, the buoy tender *Magnolia*, the 82-foot patrol boat *Point Barrow*, and two 44-foot motor lifeboats combined forces to

Last crew of San Francisco, Number 100 *poses during decommissioning ceremonies at Alameda in the spring of 1971. Commanding officer Alba Anderson stands at center. (U.S. Coast Guard)*

In a scene repeated all along America's coasts, a large navigational buoy, 40 feet in diameter, assumes responsibility for marking San Francisco's harbor entrance. Number 100 leaves her station for the final time. April, 1971. (U.S. Coast Guard)

tow a giant buoy from Yerba Buena Island out to the *San Francisco Lightship* station. The buoy was soon moored on position and began sending its robot navigational signals. As *Number 100* left her station for the last time, the *Magnolia* headed north to assist a 36-foot and a 44-foot motor lifeboat in towing a second huge buoy from Humboldt Bay to Blunts Reef. The *Blunts Reef Lightship* then upped anchor for the last time.

Many who knew the ships were deeply moved at their departure. San Francisco's *Number 100*'s master, Chief Warrant Officer Alba Anderson, said, ". . . I'm sad . . . when she leaves it's like a person dying." A former member of the *Blunts Reef* crew, Richard Mueller, helped tow its buoy out from Humboldt Bay. "When the day came to pull the buoy to Blunts Reef . . . it was like being invited to a funeral," he observed. Both lightships returned to Yerba Buena Island to the wharf at Coast Guard Base San Francisco (the new name for the old Lighthouse Depot). The ships were to have very different fates.

Blunts Reef, WLV 612, paused only briefly in San Francisco Bay and then proceeded to the East Coast where she took up station as Maine's *Portland Lightship*. Later, she became the *Nantucket Lightship*, the Atlantic seaboard's last active lightship station. She is still in use off Cape Cod.

San Francisco's *Number 100*, once the finest lightship in America, was sent to Coast Guard Base Alameda, on Government Island, near Oakland. There she was decommissioned and her name painted out, giving her a solid red hull. Instead of being preserved as a museum, as many local residents expected, *Number 100* was requisitioned by the Navy and given to the South Vietnam government. The historic lightship, its bridge still filled with gleaming brass, sailed out of the Golden Gate, bound for the Philippines. It had become yet another victim of the Vietnam War. Her fate in Southeast Asia is not known, but she may still be afloat.

Relief WLV 605 became the relief vessel for the 13th Coast Guard District, annually replacing *Columbia River Lightship, WLV 604,* the last Pacific Coast lightship station. Today, the *Nantucket* and *Columbia River* lightships are the last active light vessels in the United States.

Fortunately, groups in Oregon and Washington made concerted efforts to save three of the remaining lightships. Old *Blunts Reef, Number 83,* has been preserved by Northwest Seaport of 1143 Federal Avenue in Seattle. *Columbia River, Number 88,* a ship which never saw duty in California, has been restored by the Columbia River Maritime Museum and may be toured at Astoria, Oregon.

A third lightship, *Relief WLV 605,* was decommissioned at Seattle on December 31, 1975. This vessel is presently docked in Olympia, Washington, and plans call for the State Capitol Historical Association to use the *Relief* as a museum ship. *WLV 605*'s retirement became possible when the Coast Guard began using a buoy rather than a relief lightship to stand in for *Columbia WLV 604* when that ship returned to port for two months each summer for repairs.

Today, no lightships remain in California. For those who desire a last glimpse of an active lightship, Astoria, Oregon offers a rare opportunity. A good pair of binoculars makes it easy to pick out *Columbia River, WLV 604,* off the mouth of the Columbia. Cape Disappointment, Washington, and Fort Stevens, Oregon, provide perhaps the closest vantage points. Tours of the museum ships offer still another worth-while insight into lightship history.

Some day the First Coast Guard District of Boston will retire *WLV 612*, a ship which formerly served both at the San Francisco bar and Blunts Reef. Perhaps a reader will lead an effort to have this ship returned to California so we may regain a precious part of our maritime heritage.

U.S. Life-Saving Service breeches buoy.

HUMBOLDT HARBOUR

Humboldt Bay is the heartland of the world's tallest trees, an area rich in redwood and Douglas fir. Lumber mills rim the bay, and freighters of many nations arrive to fill their holds with wood products. Between San Francisco and Coos Bay, Oregon—a distance of four hundred nautical miles—Humboldt Bay provides the only shipping point for large, ocean-going vessels. Ever since the founding of Eureka in 1850, the bay has been one of America's major lumber ports.

Humboldt Bay is small when compared with San Francisco Bay, but mariners realize that its bar is at least as treacherous. The entrance channel is narrow, its approaches are low and difficult to see, and the North Coast's storms are more frequent at Humboldt Bay than at the Golden Gate. The *Annual Report of the United States Life-Saving Service* series chronicle more terrible shipwrecks at Humboldt Bay than at the great port to the south.

Eureka was but a year old when Congress, recognizing the potential of the harbor, appropriated $15,000 for a lighthouse to mark the entrance to Humboldt Bay. Officially called the Humboldt Harbour Light Station (and spelled in the English manner), construction of the beacon was delayed by inadequate funding, poor transportation, and problems with contractors. Five years passed before work began in 1856.

The bay's low, sandy North Spit was selected as the best site for the light. There, among the yellow lupine, workmen dug a basement and began constructing a 45-foot-high masonry tower. A one-and-a-half-story dwelling in the Cape Cod style was built at the base of the tower, completely surrounding it so that the light tower rose through the dwelling's roof. Designed by architect Ammi B. Young, seven of California's earliest lighthouses would be built in this style. This plan was used almost exclusively in California, and only in the decade between 1850 and 1860. Among the seven sentinels, Humboldt Harbour would be distinctive because of the greater height of its tower in relation to the size of the dwelling.*

In the lantern room, workers installed a fixed, white, fourth order lens. The lens was lighted by a lamp with a single, circular wick which

---

*There is some speculation by historians that the tower may have been raised during its career. There were frequent complaints from mariners that the sentinel was too low. Photographs, all taken during the beacon's later years, show an unusually tall tower for this style of lighthouse.

Humboldt Harbour lighthouse amid the sand dunes. When this photograph was taken about 1900, a long series of natural disasters had already forced its abandonment. (Clarke Museum, Eureka)

burned vegetable oil. On the evening of December 20, 1856, keeper J. Johnson climbed the winding stairs and then a ladder through the hatch into the lantern room. As the wick flickered to life, Humboldt Harbour began operation. It was a one-keeper station without a fog signal.

Interestingly, Johnson was not the station's first attendant. One D. W. Pearce had been appointed keeper two years earlier. Perhaps he tired of being a keeper without a light. At any rate, he resigned shortly before the lens arrived.

Johnson tended the beacon for three years, ably assisted by his wife, Sarah. Then keeper Johnson died. Widowed, Sarah E. Johnson became the station's lone keeper on February 25, 1859. Mrs. Johnson was one of at least fourteen women who served as California lighthouse keepers. In the days when women were denied equal employment opportunity, most could become light keepers only by succeeding a husband or father upon his death. As with all of her sister keepers, Sarah Johnson did an excellent job. She kept the white lighthouse with its red (later black) lantern room in fine condition. Her grandson, Joshua Vansant, was born in the lighthouse in November, 1861. Mrs. Johnson

While still an active station, keepers used a long boardwalk to bring supplies in from the landing. (Bancroft Library)

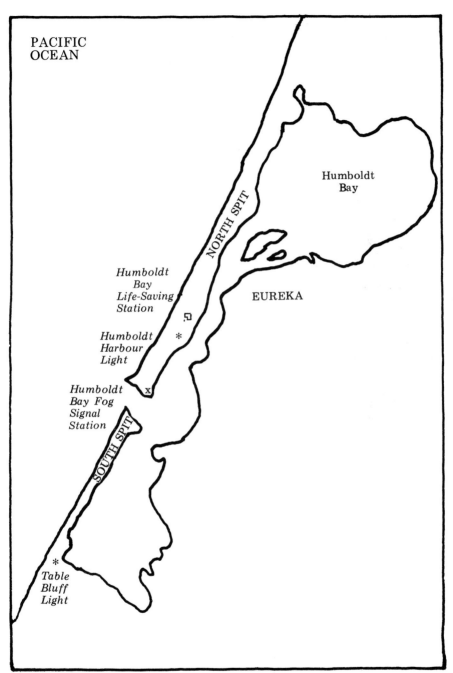

Humboldt Bay

served at Humboldt Harbour light until December, 1863. Counting the years she served with her husband, her tenure at the harsh station was longer than any of her male counterparts. One of her successors, A. P. Marble, lasted five years at the station, second longest term of service. The other men who held the post soon moved on to gentler and less isolated employment.

It is not surprising that Humboldt Harbour never attracted keepers willing to stay the twenty or thirty years that was not uncommon elsewhere. Life on the North Spit in those days was difficult and sometimes dangerous. The station stood in isolation amid shifting sand dunes. Although Eureka and Bucksport were within view, getting there during the 1850's and 1860's meant hiking through the sand, then wading out to a moored sailboat and, finally (weather and tide permitting), making an often-sloppy trip across the estuary to the city. An alternate overland route required circumventing the bay, a trek through miles of soft sand. When a gale blew in, the station was blasted by flying sand and battered by the winds. When it was calm, it was often foggy. One year over 1,100 hours of fog were logged.

It seems incredible that any station marking a harbor as fogbound as Humboldt Bay should continue to be without a fog signal well into the 1870's, but it was not until 1872 that a bell boat was acquired as a sound signal. Bell boats had been invented for use on the Atlantic Coast, beginning in 1852. Typically, they were iron-hulled boats, 30 feet long, with a 300-pound bell mounted atop a short mast. A grooved plate under the bell supported a cannon ball and, as the boat rocked and pitched, the cannon ball would roll about, ringing the bell. Such devices worked well off Boston, but winter storms on California's Redwood Coast gave local bell boats short lives. Humboldt Bay's bell boat lasted only two years.

Before the bell boat was a year old, the Lighthouse Service recognized its limited future and funds were approved for a steam fog whistle. Work began at once, and in March, 1874, the whistle began operation. Water came from three wells and, in this lumber-rich country, cordwood was chosen to fire the boilers. Tending the whistle was no small chore since it took a monumental amount of wood to blow a steam whistle for over 1,000 hours yearly.

Construction costs for the new fog signal had risen far beyond all estimates and the Lighthouse Service was less than pleased. Assistant lighthouse engineer E. G. Molera was dispatched from San Francisco, carrying a sack full of gold coins and a long list of questions.

The gold coins were to pay off the construction workers, while the list of questions was for a Mr. Fauntleroy, the contractor. Careful calculations by the Lighthouse Service staff showed that fencing the reservation would require no more than 8,000 board feet of lumber. Mr.

As the years took their toll, the dwelling portion fell away from Humboldt Harbour lighthouse, leaving its tower to stand alone. 1933. (Wayne Piland Family)

Fauntleroy had already purchased 14,000 board feet. Molera was also interested in inspecting the fog signal house. Original cost estimates had been just $3,000, yet the Service had already received bills for over $6,000. Several independent carpenters had submitted estimates that the building would require no more than 16,000 board feet of lumber to construct. Mr. Fauntleroy had bought—and used—over 58,000 board feet. The Lighthouse Service may well have been the most frugal agency in the entire Federal Government, and Headquarters was furious at the inexplicably high costs.

Molera soon discovered why the building had been so expensive. From the floor up, the fog signal building was of unusual construction. Original plans had called for an ordinary dirt floor in the wood storage room. Mr. Fauntleroy had begun with tongue-and-groove flooring. On top of this he had placed a layer of brick—laid on end—and then cemented the upright bricks firmly in place. For "added security" the entire floor had been covered with two inches of cement mortar.

History does not record engineer Molera's meeting with Mr. Fauntleroy nor do we know whether Fauntleroy had profit as a motive or rather that he was simply a man of unusually high construction standards. In any event, the whistles began blasting away on May 10, 1874, much to the relief of local mariners.

As things worked out, one wonders if Fauntleroy had an inkling of what was ahead when he decided to use his heavy-duty construction techniques. In November, 1877, an earthquake struck the station, cracking the lighthouse walls. A new boathouse, launchways, and landing had just been built to ease reaching Eureka; but the storms during the winter of 1877 were severe and the landing and boathouse were badly damaged. In 1882 still another earthquake jarred the lighthouse. Building a rigid brick beacon on a sandy spit in earthquake country was one of the Lighthouse Service's more questionable decisions.

In 1883, nature surrounded the station in an extraordinary fog. As usual when fog crept in, the boilers were stoked and the whistle began blowing. This time, however, the fog stayed and stayed. For days on end the whistle blew. Finally, after 120 hours of continuous operation, the old, upright boiler gave out and the whistle was silent.

There were tugboats on the foggy bar when the boiler failed. Without the whistle sounds to guide them, the tugs came close to wrecking. The harried wickies worked frantically, trying to restore the whistle, but it was hours before the boiler was repaired.

Humboldt Bay's bar was no place to be during thick weather, especially without a navigational aid. In 1878 the Humboldt Bay Life-Saving Station had been established by the U.S. Life-Saving Service. It was the second lifesaving station in California, the first being Golden Gate Park Station in San Francisco, opened earlier that same year. The new station was near the lighthouse, with the doors to its boat room opening to the bay. The station was equipped with the usual lifeboat, surfboat, Lyle gun, beach apparatus, breeches buoy, and the like. The station house had a lookout tower on its roof.

During thick weather and storms, surfmen patrolled the North Spit from the bar to a point about three miles north. The patrols could be dangerous. During rough weather, the sea would cut out a high sand dune between patrols. A surfman returning in the fog would come upon an unexpected, 15-foot drop. If he fell in, it was difficult to get back up the cliff and the next sea could come in and sweep him away. Surfmen walked their patrols alone, and there was no possibility of assistance. There was no shirking of duty, either. Patrolmen carried a key for the punch clocks located at the bar and at the extreme north end of the patrol. If the surfman did not punch in at each location, he was assumed not to have completed his patrol.

The life-saving station responded to countless rescue calls. Frequently, light keepers aided the surfmen, and it was not uncommon for the light-keeping family to be called upon to care for a house-full of

Surfmen from the nearby Humboldt Bay Lifeboat Station staged their breeches buoy drills near old Humboldt Harbour lighthouse. Surfmen in foreground are pulling the breeches buoy up to the man on the mast. 1924. (Carl Christensen)

Moments later, the breeches buoy reached the mast, the surfman climbed in, and he was hauled down. Such drills were weekly occurrences at all Redwood Coast life-saving stations. 1924. (Carl Christensen)

cold and hungry shipwreck victims. When word of a shipwreck spread to Eureka, newspaper reporters sometimes rushed to the lighthouse to await developments and interview survivors. A pot of hot coffee was always kept bubbling, and the keepers were renowned for their cheerful acceptance of visitors.

That the light keepers could continue to provide hospitable shelter is to their credit, especially after the events of 1885. That year the helpless station was hit by a cyclone, something almost unheard of in California. Keeper William C. Price must have been stunned as he watched the roofs fly off the lighthouse and the fog signal shed. Telephone poles were flattened and the plank walks torn up. Later in the year, during November, the beacon was assaulted again, this time by the sea. An extraordinarily high tide rose, and the sea covered much of the spit. The lighthouse was soon surrounded by water. Huge driftwood logs sloshed about and threatened to batter the beacon to pieces. Fortunately, the lighthouse held together, but when the tide finally receded, the reservation was littered with driftwood and debris. The lighthouse's cellar had been completely flooded and the structure began to settle. Cracks began appearing in the walls as the building continued to sink.

Frequent visitor to Humboldt Bay was the lighthouse tender Sequoia, *flagship of the 18th Lighthouse District's vessels. She is shown here shortly after arriving in California in 1909. (U.S. Coast Guard)*

The Lighthouse Service had suffered long enough. Since 1867 the lighthouse had been criticized as being too low and the North Spit as being so foggy that the station failed to provide adequate navigational aid. Now nearly ten years of natural disasters had forced the Lighthouse Service to decide to relocate the light and fog signal. A new station would be constructed four miles to the south on Table Bluff, a high, secure headland on the edge of Humboldt Bay. The lens would be removed from Humboldt Harbour light and placed in the new beacon on Table Bluff. A new fog whistle would be built there, too, and old Humboldt Harbour Light Station would be abandoned.

Lens lanterns were mounted on wood frames to mark the harbor entrance. On October 31, 1892, Table Bluff Light Station began operation and all duties performed at Humboldt Harbour were terminated. For some years the new facility at Table Bluff was called the Humboldt Bay Light Station, a terminology that has confused some historians. Eventually, the present title of Table Bluff Light Station came into official use.

After closure, the old beacon remained an empty daymark. During the late 1890's the old lighthouse was occupied by employees of the U.S. War Department engaged in engineering work to improve the harbor entrance and jetty. In 1906, with plans under way to build a new fog signal on the North Spit, the Lighthouse Service ordered the neglected sentinel torn down; but the action was never carried out. It continued to stand for decades. Slowly the dwelling crumbled around the tower, and by the mid-1930's only the tower remained upright.

Then, about 1933, the ancient beacon mysteriously collapsed, after nearly a half-century of neglect. Scuttlebut held that members of the local Coast Guard crew had toppled it as a prank.

Old-timers around Humboldt Bay insisted that, though abandoned, the sentinel had never been dark. They claimed its lantern room emitted a ghostly glow "all by itself" on certain nights. If so, perhaps a supernatural light was fitting for a beacon that had ended its career on Halloween Eve long ago in 1892.

TABLE BLUFF

Table Bluff lighthouse was born out of failure. Stung by mariners' criticisms that Humboldt Harbour light was too low and faced with unparalleled maintenance problems, the Lighthouse Service decided that the old beacon must be abandoned. The station had to be re-established on high, stable ground, yet be close enough to Humboldt Bay to adequately mark the harbor.

Four miles south of the Humboldt Bay bar stands 165-foot-high Table Bluff. The bluff towers above surrounding lowlands, its steep cliffs rising up from a narrow beach. Viewed from any direction Table Bluff is a prominent landmark. Besides offering solid ground for a light station, the hill overlooks both Humboldt Bay and the mouth of the Eel River. A new beacon here would serve mariners entering either the bay or the river.

The Lighthouse Service liked the site, but so did its owner, Eureka City Councilman W. S. Clark. It was only after the government threatened condemnation proceedings that Clark agreed to part with six acres atop the bluff. On March 3, 1892, the local press reported, "Bids will be received at the office of the U.S. Lighthouse Engineers . . . for construction of the new lighthouse at Table Bluff."

By the 1890's the Lighthouse Service had learned what architectural designs were well suited to California. Two stations had just been completed in southern California, and engineers drew upon the plans of each for Table Bluff. San Diego's Ballast Point light was the prototype for the lighthouse, while San Luis Obispo light station furnished the model for the assistant keepers' duplex dwelling and for the fog signal building.

The new station soon rose along the seaward edge of the dark headland. The main buildings were laid out in a line facing the sea. Northernmost was the 30-foot-high lighthouse, attached to a one-and-a-half-story dwelling which served as the home of the head keeper. The next structure to the south was the fog signal building with its steam whistles. Beyond was a double dwelling, a duplex housing the two assistant keepers and their families. Landward of these three structures stood two "wash houses" or laundries, an oil house, and a carpenter shop. The entire area was nicely set off with white picket fences and

Table Bluff was one of the most peaceful light stations on the California coast. However, an earthquake did topple the fog signal building's big chimney shown here at center. (Wallace Martin)

neatly trimmed cypress hedges. All the buildings were painted white with red roofs except the lighthouse lantern room, which was black.

The fixed, white, fourth order lens was removed from Humboldt Harbour lighthouse and installed at Table Bluff. On October 31, 1892, head keeper Tony Schmoll and his two assistants lighted the lamp for the first time. Humboldt Harbour light station ceased operation that same evening.

Initially, Table Bluff was called Humboldt *Bay* Light Station, a fact which has led some historians to confuse it with Humboldt *Harbour* Light Station. Eventually, the term "Table Bluff" was officially adopted.

In 1911 the Lighthouse Service replaced the lighthouse's old fixed lens with a new, flashing one. Both old and new lenses were of the fourth order; any larger size would have required rebuilding the lantern room.

Table Bluff would never be the scene of great storms or terrible shipwrecks, but it was not far from the Humboldt Bay bar where disaster struck with alarming regularity. The keepers had orders, therefore, "to warn the life-saving crew when vessels are in distress," by sounding five or six short, sharp blasts followed by a prolonged 15-second blast

Table Bluff Light Station. Dwelling is at far left, fog signal building at center, and the lighthouse at right. Flat-roofed building is the oil house. To the left of the oil house is the carpenter shop. (Esther Gonzales)

with the fog whistle. This means of communication was supplemented (but not replaced) by a telephone line completed in 1901.

In 1906 the Navy established a radio sending and receiving station at Table Bluff. Later the Navy would build a radio compass station here, too. This gave the light keepers some new neighbors as well as providing mariners with new means of securing assistance.

In 1921, in a terrible maritime disaster, the passenger steamer *Alaska* went down on Blunts Reef. Ironically, at the very moment the ship sent its distress call, Table Bluff radio station was handling another message and the urgent call was missed. Fortunately, a nearby ship picked up the call and eventually word reached Table Bluff. It was the radio station's role to handle marine radio messages and then to notify Humboldt Bay Coast Guard by telephone. It was a roundabout communications method, but it was a vast improvement over the earlier system of burning a flare or blowing the fog signal.

Carl Christensen, substitute surfman at Humboldt Bay Lifeboat Station, still recalls the scene when his motor lifeboat arrived at Blunts Reef. Survivors were floating about in the fog on life rafts and on pieces of wreckage. The surfmen gathered the living first, transferring them to a steamer. Then the motor lifeboat picked her way through the wreckage gathering bodies. It was a long, dreary run back to Eureka where the boatload of bodies was put ashore. Ironically, the wreck had occurred just a short distance from the *Blunts Reef Lightship.* Had the vessel been equipped with a radio, all those on board the *Alaska* might have been saved. Table Bluff's radio station could not be of maximum benefit until all ships carried radio equipment.

Young Stephen Pozanac arrived at Table Bluff light in 1922. During World War I he had been stationed at Fort Barry in Marin County. There he became acquainted with lighthouse keepers from Point Bonita. Pozanac was impressed with their life style and determined that, after the war, he would become a wickie. A ride on an Army ferryboat from San Francisco helped firm his goal. On the boat he met Minnie Diflivson, daughter of Lime Point light keeper Peter Diflivson. Mr. Diflivson liked Lime Point enough to stay there twenty-seven years, and Minnie liked Stephen Pozanac enough to marry him. Joining the Lighthouse Service, they spent their first three years at lonely Año Nuevo Island. They spent the next sixteen at Table Bluff.

The young couple enjoyed their life on the south shore of Humboldt Bay. The Pozanacs even found that there was time to run a small outside business. They used the six-acre reservation to raise great quantities of chickens and vegetables. So successful was this enterprise that they eventually came to supply a number of Eureka grocery stores with fryers, eggs, and produce. Table Bluff wasn't the most exciting station on the Redwood Coast, but it was one of the most productive.

Table Bluff entrance gate was typical of many California light stations. (Esther Gonzales)

Table Bluff's fog signal building, and to the left the wireless antenna. 1945. (U.S. Coast Guard)

Still, Table Bluff had its thrilling moments. The keepers stood watch in the fog signal building. One night when it was first assistant Pozanac's turn to go on watch, he made his way from the duplex toward the fog signal building. Suddenly, he felt a jolt, and with a great crash all of the station's lights went dark. An earthquake had struck, toppling the tall chimney of the fog signal building. The chimney had crashed through the building's roof, landing in a massive pile exactly where Pozanac was to stand watch. Had the tremor struck a few moments later, it would have been the assistant keeper's last watch.

As it was, the Pozanacs left Table Bluff in 1938, transferring to Ballast Point. The transition must have been an unusually easy one, since both lighthouses were identical.

Pozanac was succeeded by Wallace "Wally" Evans, who soon rose to be head keeper. Evans was assisted by Earl Mayeau and Ray Gonzales. Evans and Mayeau had served at such difficult stations as the Farallons and Mile Rocks during their earlier years. Gonzales and his wife, Esther, had been at Fort Point, beneath the Golden Gate bridge. Indeed, their house had been moved two times to give place to the cable anchorage of the huge bridge.

In 1940 Table Bluff was still a quiet place. Twice a day the Blunts Reef lightship was contacted by radio telephone to assure that all was secure at the light vessel. The Navy's two tall radio towers occasionally received exciting news. But, generally, life was slow and relaxed. Then World War II began.

Table Bluff's position made the station ideal as a major base for the Beach Patrol. A large barracks for single men and six quarters for married people were constructed on the grounds. Table Bluff's beach patrolmen guarded the coast on horseback, ranging from the Humboldt Bay entrance south to the mouth of the Eel River. A coastal lookout was also estabalished to take advantage of the bluff's commanding view.

With light keepers, Navy radio men, radio compass station operators, Coast Guard beach patrolmen, and coastal lookouts all living at Table Bluff, the station reached its peak expansion. An unanticipated side effect of the war was to be the destruction of most of the older buildings.

When the war ended, Table Bluff had many excess buildings. About 1948 the Coast Guard began eliminating some of the empty structures. Only the light keepers had stayed on when the war ended. They were moved into newer homes once used by the officers' families at the Navy radio station. The old double dwelling was razed along with many lesser structures. Especially unfortunate was the removal of the dwelling portion of the lighthouse. When the demolition project was over, the light tower stood alone. With the supporting walls of the residence gone, cables had to be installed to help hold the lighthouse upright.

Snow on the coast. By the time this January, 1950 picture was taken, the Coast Guard had dismantled the dwelling portion of the lighthouse. The solitary tower still stands today. (Esther Gonzales)

There was, however, still a need for the beacon, and Table Bluff's old lens and diaphone fog horns continued to serve navigators. At 6 o'clock one morning in June, 1948, Esther Gonzales answered a knock at her door. It was a commercial fisherman in need of help. His boat, the *Pollyanna*, had gone ashore during the night on Humboldt Bay's South Spit. At daybreak the fisherman had hiked to the light station. Saving his boat was no easy task, but using a Coast Guard cutter, a bulldozer, a jeep, and a crew to haul on a line, the light keepers and the Coast Guardsmen refloated the vessel. It was probably the last shipwreck for Table Bluff light, for the era of light keepers on the bluff was coming to a close.

In 1953 the fog signal was discontinued and the light automated and unmanned. Eventually, a group of young people obtained the reservation for use as a religious community. They called their new home "Lighthouse Ranch."

As late as 1972, the now automated lighthouse remained in use. Coast Guardsmen from Humboldt Bay station periodically serviced the sentinel, mingling amicably with the members of the communal group.

When the lighthouse tenders weren't hauling supplies to isolated light stations and lightships, they were often tied up at Lighthouse Depot wharf on Yerba Buena Island. From left can be seen the Madroño, the Sequoia, and the Blunts Reef Lightship, Number 83. July 4, 1922. (U.S. Coast Guard)

Lighthouse tender Lupine brought supplies to Humboldt Bay. Here, in June, 1927, the Lupine takes on provisions at Pier 15 in San Francisco prior to a supply run along the California coast. (U.S. Coast Guard)

However, establishment of powerful, new range lights at the Humboldt Bay entrance meant that the old light was no longer needed. The old sentinel now stands dark, amid vegetable gardens and children.

Fittingly, the new range lights flash just a few hundred yards from the site of the original Humboldt Harbour lighthouse. Perhaps those who long ago chose the North Spit as the best lighthouse site have finally been proven right.

Table Bluff lighthouse may be seen by turning off U.S. Highway 101 onto Hookton Road, between Loleta and Fields Landing. Follow Hookton west as it becomes Table Bluff Road. When the road climbs the bluff and passes through a cluster of old military buildings, the reservation has been reached. Table Bluff lighthouse is to the left, clearly visible from several places along the road.

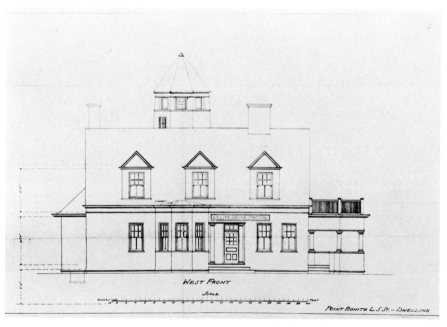

Point Bonita Life-Saving Station—original plan. C. 1900. (R. Shanks)

The self-righting lifeboat.

Launching the surfboat.

HUMBOLDT BAY

Relocating the light from Humboldt Bay's entrance to Table Bluff had proven a reasonably good idea. The new lighthouse could guide mariners toward the bay and then minor harbor lights would mark the entrance itself. However, placing the fog signal four miles from the bar had been a mistake. By 1900 the Lighthouse Service was sure that it again needed a fog signal at the old location. Congress was told, "There are three lights (two lens lanterns and a post light) maintained on the jetties to guide vessels over the bar. These, however, are ineffective in thick or foggy weather by day or night. It is evident that a fog signal is much needed here."

In 1908 a fog signal station was established at the very tip of the north jetty. Its keeper, George D. Cobb, and his assistant, Peter Admiral, presided over 197 acres of shifting sands with an average elevation of just ten feet above mean low water.

Since they operated a fog signal station, there was no lighthouse to tend. But as at one or two other fog signal stations, minor harbor lights had to be kept filled with oil and lighted regularly. Eventually, harbor light tending would evolve into a major duty at Humboldt Bay, and a three-man crew would be required at the station.

George Cobb was to have a long and notable career at Humboldt Bay. In 1916 the Lighthouse Board cited both Cobb and his new assistant, T. S. Thompson, for bravery. A Navy submarine stranded just off the North Spit while a terrible surf was running. Rigging a breeches buoy and evacuating the submarine's crew had proven dangerous and difficult. However, through the combined efforts of the Humboldt Bay Lifeboat Station's surfmen and the two keepers, all hands were saved; although the Navy was to lose the cruiser *Milwaukee* during subsequent efforts to pull the submarine free.

By 1919 Humboldt Bay's fog signal station had become an attractive installation. Twin, one-and-a-half-story, seaside bungalows stood facing the harbor entrance. With gables, coal-fired stoves, and sun porches, the frame dwellings were comfortable abodes for the keeper and his first assistant and their families. A walkway supported the plank rails of a tramway with its little flatcar. (The keepers called the car a "push car," since they did the pushing when supplies came ashore.) The tramway-walkway ran from the station's dock at one end to the fog

Humboldt Bay fog signal station was at the very edge of the harbor entrance. Fog signal building is at left while keeper's and first assistant's dwellings are at right. Note ornamental hedges. C. 1939. (U.S. Coast Guard)

Humboldt Bay's fog signal building housed air sirens. 1921. (U.S. Coast Guard)

Interior of the fog signal building held (left to right) gasoline engine, air compressor, and air tanks—the equipment necessary to power the air sirens. 1921. (U.S. Coast Guard)

signal building at the other, passing by the front yards of the residences. A carpenter shop and oil house stood near the fog signal. Twin, compressed-air sirens projected from the fog signal building's roof, powered by hand-cranked gasoline engines located inside the structure.

The only flaw in the station was its location, which was merely a sand dune just above sea level at the edge of a rough bar. Storm waves tore at the dunes and only a small bulkhead prevented seas from washing into the keepers' front yards. The oil house was farther seaward and more exposed. The Pacific swept away its sandy foundation, and the oil house tilted into the water. By 1920 a substantial new bulkhead had to be built or the station would have ended up in the middle of the bar, along with the hulks of wrecked ships. Eroding sand had been a recurrent problem at stations on the low Atlantic seaboard, but it was an uncommon problem on the high, rocky Pacific Coast.

As the duties of tending harbor lights increased, another keeper, called the second assistant, was assigned to the station. He took up residence in a two-story, frame house a half mile away. Located near the lifeboat station and the abandoned lighthouse, it looked like a very substantial farmhouse. It remained from the days of the old lighthouse and had reportedly been a part of the early station. Although not close to the fog signal, it was a fine place to live. When Wayne Piland, his wife, Martha, and young children, Nancy and Donald, moved into the big house in 1932, they were impressed. Besides a well-fenced yard with redwood deck, they had their own carpenter shop, garden area, chicken house, engine house, well, water tank, and shed. In front of their home was the old lighthouse dock with a boat shed and power launch. Alongside the dock was a coal house and oil house. It was quite an array of buildings to be placed at one's disposal after only six months in the Lighthouse Service.

The Pilands' immediate neighbors were the Coast Guard crew and their families. The Coast Guard station's officer-in-charge, Garner Churchill, his wife, Thora, and their children lived in the green cottage adjacent to the lifeboat station. Churchill and his crew guarded California's most dangerous harbor entrance, and he required the best from his men. Chief Churchill had begun his career here, served two years at Fort Point Lifeboat Station on San Francisco Bay, and returned to become commanding officer. He inspired confidence and dedication in crews; when a distress call came, his entire crew would dash to the motor lifeboat, hoping to be chosen to go with him. He drilled his men repeatedly—on the beach, in the surf, and during classes held in the station. His men were the Pacific Coast champions in the Coast Guard pulling boat races. During his years at Humboldt, he and his crew would save over three hundred lives.

Dwellings of the keeper and his first assistant. A tramway runs in front of the residences. 1921. (U.S. Coast Guard)

Second assistant keeper's dwelling. Fog signal station's keepers reported mysterious footsteps here. 1921. (U.S. Coast Guard)

To the north of the Lighthouse Wharf (beyond the granite chips remaining from the great stone blocks that had been cut for St. George Reef light), three surfmen, veterans of the old Life-Saving Service, and their families lived in little houses along the beach. The most experienced surfman was Ole Torgerson, who had served since the days of pulling boats and life cars, when beach carts were hauled by men. Torgerson and two other Scandinavian surfmen, all now middle-aged, remained active members of the lifeboat station's crew. These highly-skilled civilians had seen their station equipped with California's first power lifeboat in 1905. The old class "E" 36-footer was still in use in the 1930's and continued to perform well.

Prohibition was now in effect; and on moonless nights when the bar was smooth, the deep roar of a high-powered motorboat could be heard as rum runners dashed out over the bar in the darkness. Two of the lumber ships that frequently called at Eureka caught the attention of those living on the North Spit. The ships would slip in and out of the harbor without the customary notice in the local newspapers, and their crews "looked like pirates" to the surfmen and light keepers. When Federal agents finally captured one of the ships, they found cases of illegal liquor beneath the stacks of Redwood Coast lumber.

Humboldt Bay was a very busy harbor in the 1930's, and increased shipping required that the fog signal station's keepers tend a growing number of small navigational aids. At the end of the jetty there was a large gas accumulator light, a difficult beacon to reach when waves washed the jetty. Inside the harbor were several additional gas accumulator lights and lens lanterns, but most channels were marked by simple kerosene-burning post lanterns. The post lanterns hung from piles and each had a large copper reservoir on top which fed the lamp its oil. The reservoirs held enough kerosene to burn for five or six days, but the keepers always refilled them every third day so that there would be little chance for the light to run dry.

When the wickies took their power launch (they nearly always worked in pairs) to tend the lights that marked the channel into Eureka, wives from the stations would often go along so that they could shop in town. The trip could often be a frustrating one for all concerned. As the keepers worked their way from one light to another, they approached each post lantern stern first, one man throwing a line around the supporting pile and the other easing in the boat so that the boat was gently secured to the post. If their timing was off, the boat would hit the pile with a jar, showering everyone with kerosene. While the women tried to wipe their "go to town" dresses clean, the rope that held the lantern was uncleated and the lantern and reservoir were lowered to the boat. The reservoir was filled with oil, but before it could be placed back atop the lantern, the light had to be opened and its wick trimmed or replaced. The keepers would then relight the wick, pausing to insure that it was burning properly, without "fish tail," or lop-sided, flame. The reservoir would then be replaced and the entire unit hauled back up, to hang from the top of the post. The party would then shove off toward the next post light, and, ultimately, Eureka.

The Humboldt Bay fog signal station attendants had an assistant, an old "lamp lighter," who tended the post lanterns on northeastern Humboldt Bay from Arcata Dock down to Eureka. A part-time Lighthouse Service employee for longer than anyone could remember, each morning he rowed to work in Eureka, putting out the lamps along the way. At day's end, he spent the evening rowing back to Arcata, relighting the lanterns as he progressed toward home.

The most difficult light to service was the south jetty light. Located far out on a cement and rock jetty subject to heavy spray and often covered with slippery marine plants and animals, it was hard and dangerous work for Wayne Piland and John McGrath as they carried bulky accumulators out to supply power for the light. Keepers frequently fell, sometimes dropping the accumulator. The possibility of an unexpectedly large sea sweeping the men off the jetty was always present.

Fog signal station's attendants had to maintain many small harbor lights of which this one was typical. 1920. (U.S. Coast Guard)

Humboldt Bay Life-Saving Station was the second rescue station built in California. Note launchways in foreground and lookout tower on the roof. Above the open doors of the boat room can be seen the windows and gables of the upstairs room where surfmen slept while on call. 1930. (Mr. and Mrs. Garner Churchill)

Upstairs sleeping room at Humboldt Bay Life-Saving Station. Ladder leads up to the lookout tower. 1924. (Carl Christensen)

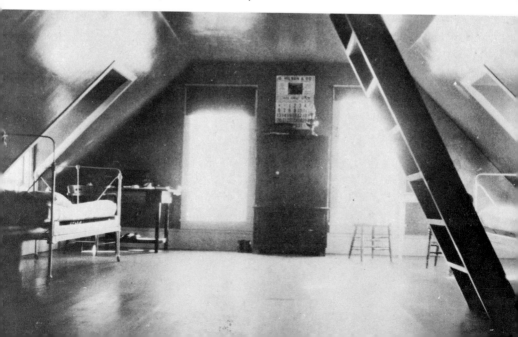

The light was an important one. The big steel mast of the old passenger steamer *Corona* still rose from the sand after she had come to her end nearby in 1907. When the steam schooner *Brooklyn* was lost on the bar in 1930, all but one on board had perished. Then in the first months of 1932, unusually severe storms hit and gigantic waves swept the bar. By mid-January, sea conditions were so severe that an almost unprecedented thing happened. Due to the terrible seas sweeping the jetty, the fog signal station crew found the south jetty light completely inaccessible. The keepers had no choice but to allow the light to go out. Three nights later, the lumber steamer *Tiverton* arrived off the harbor entrance. Despite continued foul weather, an attempt was made to cross the bar. A red light could be seen, and the *Tiverton*'s officers assumed that it must be the south jetty light. As the ship came in, the confused vessel suddenly made a sharp turn and stranded on the sand spit. The flashing red light was not the south jetty light, now darkened, but a buoy flashing far inside the bay.

The Coast Guard responded immediately. Chief Garner Churchill, despite illness, led his men across the bar in two motor lifeboats. Once there, they found the *Tiverton* aground, about one thousand feet offshore. The *Tiverton* was a well-built ship, and she survived a night of pounding seas, her crew still aboard. By morning she had been driven far inshore, and it became clear that the rescue would have to be staged from the beach. She was now but one hundred feet out from the jetty. At 7 a.m. Churchill and his men fired their Lyle gun, hurling a line out to the *Tiverton*. A breeches buoy was rigged, and soon the crew was being hauled ashore. All were saved.

It became apparent, as the *Tiverton* came farther inshore, that the freighter would become a total loss. As the seas calmed later that day, it became possible to unload her cargo, much of it coffee. Salvors began stripping the ship, stacking her cargo on the jetty. It was still raining and blowing hard, and toward the end of the day the salvors decided to leave their cargo on the jetty for the night. Chief Churchill warned them that they were making a serious mistake as the seas were building. By that evening, there was a row of coffee cans strung along the beach for over two miles.

Word that the *Tiverton*'s cargo had come ashore spread along the North Spit. In just an hour, the beach was stripped. Later, the *Tiverton* would settle in her sandy grave, but the day's events would be discussed over many cups of hot coffee long afterward.

Barely a month later the steam schooner *Yellowstone* suffered a fate similar to the *Tiverton*'s. While crossing the turbulent bar, her stern

Stranded steam schooner Tiverton *met her doom beside Humboldt Bay's south jetty. Note breeches buoy rescue in progress. 1933. (Wayne Piland Family)*

This lookout tower was maintained at Humboldt Bay's harbor entrance. Surfmen kept a constant watch over the bar and beaches. 1924. (Carl Christensen)

Life car drill at Humboldt Bay Life-Saving Station in 1925. Life cars were still another rescue device. Designed to pass through surf too high to allow use of a breeches buoy, they could be drawn between ships and shore in much the same manner as a breeches buoy. Survivors must have experienced the world's roughest "submarine" ride. (Mr. and Mrs. Garner Churchill)

was stove in as she was smashed against the south jetty. Placed under tow, the steam schooner managed to limp into harbor, only to settle on the beach in front of the lifeboat station. In those days, the Pilands and the Churchills literally had shipwrecks in their front yards.

Starting in 1936, the Coast Guard rebuilt its Humboldt Bay Lifeboat Station. Designed in a New England, gabled architectural style derived from the stations of the old Life-Saving Service, Humboldt Bay was one of the last of the traditional rescue stations to be built, and it represented the apex of its type. A launchways led up to a three-stall boat room designed to hold 36-foot motor lifeboats and smaller surfboats. Directly above the boat room were the crew's quarters, while the officer-in-charge and his family made their home at the building's south end. The station's north end held the galley and day room. At the very top was a lookout tower. When the new station was completed in 1937, it stood proudly, immediately to the south of the original life-saving station. The old station was then razed, as was an auxiliary boathouse near the ocean beach. The old lookout tower near the north jetty was retained.

The new station was to carry on in the notable manner of its predecessor. When the yacht *Reta* capsized on the bar, Garner Churchill and his crew piloted their 36-foot motor lifeboat through heavy breakers to rescue the *Reta*'s four crewmen. For their bravery, the Coast Guard awarded its silver life-saving medal to the Humboldt Bay lifeboat crew and offered the gold medal to Churchill. Chief Churchill refused to accept any medal other than the one given his crew.

By 1940 John S. McGrath was still head keeper of the Humboldt Bay fog signal station. Through the 1930's the station had been run with the highest standards. When machinist mate Hank Mostovoy wandered down from the Coast Guard station one day, he was told he have to take off his shoes before entering the spotless fog signal building. To this day, visitors recall that the old keepers kept their stations so clean that it was literally possible to eat off the floors.

By now the fog signal station no longer had a second assistant keeper, and Coast Guardsmen lived in the old residence once occupied by Lighthouse Service families. Perhaps they didn't know it was haunted.

One night, years earlier, the second assistant keeper and his wife sat together talking at the kitchen table by the light of an oil lamp. The dwelling's front door was very large, made of heavy oak, kept secure by a great, old, brass lock. The door was hard to open and rarely used since another door was more convenient.

That lonely night, as the lamp flame burned high, the keeper and his wife talked. Upstairs their children slept peacefully. Suddenly, something came *through* the front door, not by opening it, but by

Life-Saving Service capsize drill on Humboldt Bay. C. pre-1915. (Carl Christensen)

Coast Guard capsize drills continued early tradition using this surfboat. C. 1940. (Mr. and Mrs. Garner Churchill)

passing through the oak planks. The startled couple heard nothing as the "thing" passed through the door, but as the force entered, the table lamp's flame bent way over—as if a wind were blowing it. Then, to the parents' horror, they heard slow, regulated steps climb the stairs toward their children's room. The couple could hardly breathe and for a moment just sat there, staring at each other in fright. As the steps passed up the stairs, the lamp flame slowly righted itself.

The keeper then picked up the lamp, placing his hand up to the chimney to prevent a draft from blowing it out—but there was no more draft. The keeper and his wife checked the front door; it was tightly closed, as always, locked securely with the old brass key unturned. The parents then cautiously went upstairs. As they expected, their children were safe, and a careful search through closets, under beds, and the like showed that no one was there.

What had happened? Whether a ghost had passed through or merely some strange wind force depends on the reader's choice of explanatory theories. Whatever the cause, similar stories are told of light stations at Yerba Buena Island, Crescent City, and St. George Reef, among others. Some, such as the foregoing account, are unquestionably true, for they are reported by some of the most responsible light-keeping families. Whether the causes are natural or supernatural is an open question, but the occurrence of mysterious sounds, identical to measured footsteps, has been an actual event at some light stations.

World War II brought a more concrete threat. At 4:20 on the afternoon of December 20, 1941, the Naval Radio Station at Table Bluff received the following message: STEAMSHIP EMIDIO OFF BLUNTS REEF LIGHTSHIP NEED ASSISTANCE AT ONCE. Coastal lookouts at Cape Mendocino, Table Bluff, Humboldt Bay, and on board the *Blunts Reef Lightship* were immediately placed on alert. An hour and fifteen minutes later a second message arrived stating that the tanker *Emidio* had been torpedoed off Blunts Reef. The message read: EMIDIO LAUNCHED LIFEBOATS. EXPLOSION IN STEM OF SHIP. SIGHTED TORPEDO TRACK .. CONTACTED LIFEBOATS 52 MEN IN WATER 2 MEN KILLED 1 DYING ... OFF CAPE MENDOCINO.

The Coast Guard cutter *Shawnee* was ordered to proceed to the rescue, but adverse weather made it doubtful that the cutter could cross the bar. Visibility varied from two hundred yards down to near zero, rain squalls blew in, and there were strong currents on the bar and around the ends of the jetty. Worse, the navigational aids were blacked out and the bar was very rough with heavy breakers. Garner Churchill concurred with Navy officials: the *Shawnee* could not cross the bar safely. Churchill wanted to try crossing the bar in his 36-foot motor lifeboat, a boat designed for such conditions, but a Navy commander

Humboldt Bay Life-Saving Station's "Class E," 36-foot, motor lifeboat, probably the first power lifeboat on the West Coast. "Captain" Garner Churchill stands at right. C. 1930. (Mr. and Mrs. Garner Churchill)

Garner Churchill receiving national life-saving medal for valor on the Humboldt Bay bar. His crew, at right, were similarly decorated. 1939. (Mr. and Mrs. Garner Churchill)

overruled him. Still, the thought of those merchant seamen off Blunts Reef plagued Churchill. Something had to be done.

Finally, Chief Churchill could stand it no longer. He telephoned the Navy commander informing him that the Coast Guard was going to the rescue. If he made it across the bar, Churchill would burn a flare to let the commander know they were safe. He then hung up.

Manning motor lifeboat number 4468, Churchill and four of his men cast off. They crossed the bar safely, burned their flare, and proceeded south at eight knots toward the disaster. It was now just after one o'clock in the morning and the sea was very rough.

About two hours later, off the mouth of the Eel River, the bow lookout reported a large, unlighted object looming up off the port bow. It proved to be a long, low and rakish ship without masts, stack or housing, its bow pointed north. The 36-footer drifted closer, to within one hundred yards of the strange vessel. Using their searchlight, the Coast Guardsmen attempted to signal the stranger, but the ship did not respond and no lights were shown. Then, as the motor lifeboat was preparing to pull away, the dark vessel began to move. Churchill headed the lifeboat northeast at a slow speed and the vessel followed. The chief had begun to have serious doubts about this strange ship. As he advanced the motor lifeboat to full speed, it was clear that the dark ship was following them, overtaking their little boat rapidly. It then became a chase and soon barely fifty yards separated the craft. Churchill now realized that the dark ship was planning to ram him.

Then the great ocean swells came to Churchill's aid. While the lifeboat was in the trough of a wave, he decided to "take evasive action." He allowed the ship to follow him until her bow was right above the lifeboat, on the crest of a wave. At that instant Churchill was in the wave's trough and he turned the boat's wheel hard to starboard. For a moment the motor lifeboat was invisible to the ship. A tremendous trailing sea gave Churchill's boat an added burst of speed and he whipped the lifeboat around so that it hove to, pointing in the opposite direction as the dark vessel. For a moment the strange ship was silhouetted against the distant glow of Eureka's lights. The mysterious craft was a Japanese submarine.

After losing the submarine, Churchill and his men again proceeded south and reached the torpedoed *Emidio*. They found no survivors, and lacking a radio, they would learn only later that surviving crewmen were safely aboard the *Blunts Reef Lightship*.

At 8:30 that morning, the Coast Guardsmen decided to return to Humboldt Bay, and they left the abandoned tanker. The return trip was slow and very wet; a heavy chop was throwing solid water on board the open motor lifeboat. An hour later, the Coast Guardsmen saw a periscope. It was heading toward them. Disregarding the sea conditions, the

The Coast Guard's seagoing tug Comanche *is based at Humboldt Bay. She and her sister ship, the* Modoc *at Coos Bay, respond to rescue calls from vessels far offshore. 1977. (R. Shanks)*

"36" began running at full speed, on a shifting course. Then the periscope disappeared.

Fifteen minutes later the periscope reappeared and began following the lifeboat as she progressed toward Eureka. Inexplicably, the periscope was suddenly pulled down, disappearing beneath the Pacific. For the remainder of the voyage, the motor lifeboat was alone.

Both Garner Churchill and the *Emidio* reached harbor. Churchill brought his boat and crew safely back across the bar. The *Emidio*, despite being torpedoed, drifted north into Crescent City harbor. As sea conditions improved, the cutter *Shawnee* was sent out to retrieve the tanker's crew from the lightship and bring them into the Navy base that had been established on the North Spit for the duration of the war.

Humboldt Bay Coast Guard Lifeboat Station as it appears today. Built to replace the old life-saving station, this magnificent structure represents the apex of Coast Guard architecture. Note traditional launchways in foreground, large doors opening to boat room, and lookout tower atop roof. 1977. (R. Shanks)

As World War II ended and passed into the following decades, the fog signal station was closed and its buildings vanished just as had the old Humboldt Harbour lighthouse. Today, only the beautiful lifeboat station still remains as a symbol of Humboldt Bay's maritime heritage.

But the feel of the North Spit and of Humboldt Bay itself today remains traditional. Take the harbor tour on the old *Madaket* and then drive to Samoa on the North Spit, through the yellow lupine to the historic Humboldt Bay Coast Guard station. By contacting the Coast Guard group commander, tours can sometimes be arranged. Stand in the old boat room and look at a life ring bearing the name *Reta*, memento of the rescue that earned silver life-saving medals. Then, after touring the station, walk out to the bar and stand among the old Monterey cypress trees. These gnarled trees are all that remain of the Humboldt Bay Fog Signal Station. They were once part of a neat hedge, carefully trimmed into arches leading to the dwellings. Finally, cross the sand to the ocean beach, out along the jetty beyond the boiler from an old shipwreck. This is where Wayne Piland and his fellow keepers risked their lives servicing the jetty light and where Garner Churchill and his crews crossed California's worst bar in the foulest weather. This is a place that required the best men had to give. It received the best from some of the finest men.

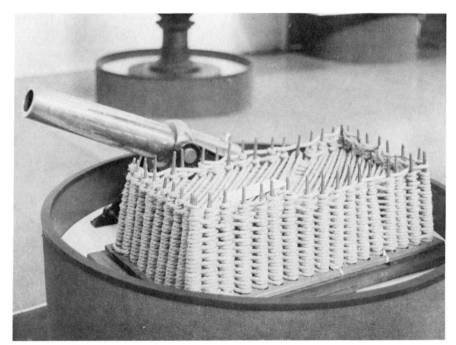

Lyle gun and faking box. (R. Shanks)

Coast Guard 36-foot motor lifeboat departs Humboldt Bay in search of rum-runners. Coxswain is Gustav Christensen. April, 1924. (Carl Christensen)

TRINIDAD HEAD

Sandy beaches extend north from Humboldt Bay for seventeen miles, culminating in Trinidad Head, a steep, rounded headland that is almost an island. The promontory is covered with a lush growth of dark green shrubs, an impressive sight outlined against the blue Pacific. Only a narrow, sandy neck connects this would-be island to the continent. It is probably the most prominent and easily-identified headland north of Cape Mendocino.

In the lee of the head is a small cove, safe when the winds blow from the northwest, but dangerous when a southwester approaches. The cove's many rocks are outnumbered by the sea birds and fishing boats that rise and fall near the wharf. There is no more scenic port on all the West Coast. The harbor exists because of the promontory. Trinidad Head is nearly 400 feet high and is almost a half-mile long and nearly as wide. On its southwest side stands Trinidad Head Light Station, home of the point's only human inhabitants.

Since the days when the Yurok Indians braved the ocean in their dugout canoes, Trinidad was important to those who went down to the sea; but if the Yurok were content to go to sea only by day, the white man was not. Beginning in 1854, there was agitation for a lighthouse at Trinidad Head. Other harbors found Congress responsive to their pleas, but it was not until 1866 that forty-two acres were purchased for the purpose of building a light station on the blunt, seaward face of Trinidad Head. It was some years later before $20,000 was approved for the necessary buildings, and it would not be until the spring of 1871 that work would even begin.

A wagon road had to be dug along the face of the head and out to the point's tip, where a narrow shelf was carved out of the rock. At the very edge of a 175-foot-high cliff, workmen built a tiny, 25-foot-high, brick lighthouse. The tower walls were painted white, while the lantern room, gallery, and trim were all done in black. Inside, a fourth order lens was installed, an appropriate light for a beacon serving a small port. A beautiful, white, frame dwelling with contrasting red roof and stylish porches was constructed 150 feet to the southeast of the light. It was a small lighthouse and a small station. For the present, there would not even be a fog signal. However, when the station's pioneer keeper, Jeremiah Kiler, first lighted the lamp on December 1, 1871, it must have

An early view of lovely Trinidad Head lighthouse. What may have been the largest wave in American history occurred here in 1913. (Humboldt State University Library)

While a keeper poses outside Trinidad Head light's lantern room, his family watches below. (Humboldt State University Library)

The beautiful keepers' dwelling at Trinidad Head. Originally the single-family dwelling shown here, it was later expanded into a double dwelling using the same architectural style. Several of the light keepers' children were born here. C. 1908. (U.S. Coast Guard)

been an act performed with pride and satisfaction. Trinidad Head was to be both a scenic and useful light for decades to come. It would be Kiler's home for the next seventeen years.

Care of the light would pass through Kiler's hands and on to his successor before Trinidad Head would be equipped with a fog signal. Finally, after twenty-six years without a sound signal, a 4,000-pound, bronze fog bell arrived in 1898. Installing it was no easy task. Construction workers once again cut a small shelf atop a 126-foot-high cliff and erected a concrete gallows to hold the giant bell out over the water. The bell was struck by a large hammer activated every ten seconds by a timer, a clockwork-driven mechanism powered by weights. As originally built, the weights hung suspended over the sea, descending the cliff face as the drum on the timer unwound. When the weights were well down the cliff, the keeper had to rewind them so that the bell would continue to ring. The timer, hammer, and bell were all protected from the weather by the frame bell house built to surround them. The addition of the bell probably occasioned assigning an assistant keeper to help with the increased duties.

The bell began ringing on July 15, 1898. Two years later there was a disaster of sorts. The wire weight cable snapped and the weights made a non-stop, 126-foot trip down to the sea. Recovery was impossible, and presumably a keeper had to ring the bell by hand until the weather cleared.

The Lighthouse Service replaced the weights, but chose a more secure method of suspension. A wooden weight tower was built on a small, concrete foundation next to the bell house. It was necessary for the skeleton weight tower to be securely mounted, not only because of high winds but also due to the fact that fog bells produce very strong vibrations when struck. These vibrations commonly caused the timers to malfunction. When that occurred, a keeper was expected to pound the bell by hand, a grueling ordeal often lasting for hours. To minimize such a possibility, Trinidad Head's bell house and tower were securely built. Warren Watkins, one of the workers, even went over the edge of the cliff and dangled from a rope while he drilled the holes necessary to anchor the tower to the rock.

There were many recurrent chores that kept the keepers busy. Running up and down the sloping boardwalk and the 48 wooden steps that led from the dwelling to the bell house and climbing the vertical ladder into the lantern room made up only part of the keepers' workload. There was, for instance, the problem of obtaining water. It was only a mile into the village of Trinidad; but it could be a steep and strenuous trek when the water supply ran low and all the station's water had to be hauled in by wagon. Anticipating the heavy winter rains, the Lighthouse Service had designed the dwelling roof to serve as the catch basin, with the run-off to flow into storage tanks. An additional 10,000-gallon tank had been added in 1890; but in some years rainfall was insufficient, and hauling water became a major task. Eventually, one of the wickies, M. Cady, discovered a spring which supplemented the roof-top supply; but it would be well into the 1930's before a pump would be installed at the spring. During the intervening years, whenever the supply ran low, keepers hauled by hand all the fresh water required for household use.

In a sense, the water problem was the outcome of manning a station only equipped with a fog bell. If the Lighthouse Service had chosen to upgrade the facility with a steam fog signal, much more water would have been required. Then it would have been necessary to provide an adequate water system. So long as the inconvenience was only human and did not affect navigational safety, the Lighthouse Service tolerated it.

The winter of 1900-1901 well illustrates the variety of problems faced by keepers at Trinidad Head. That season the roadway across the low neck to the mainland became covered by sand that drifted up from the beach. This roadway had to be kept open if the station was to function. A heavy storm washed out the sewer system and damaged a fence. On the whole, however, the keepers considered Trinidad Head a

Teddy Roosevelt's "Great White Fleet" used Trinidad Head lighthouse as a day-mark. 1908. (Ralph Hunter)

desirable station to serve at, with much excellent weather in which to tackle the rather minor damage wreaked by occasional storms.

Supplies arrived by lighthouse tender, and the sight of the *Madroño* steaming into the cove was a familiar one. The Lighthouse Service owned a wharf in Trinidad Harbor, but it was much easier to land supplies on the sandy beach between the head and the mainland. Consequently, the wharf was leased out for other uses.

Jeremiah Kiler retired as keeper in 1888 and was replaced by Fred L. Harrington, who continued the careful maintenance of the lens, with its unusual fixed and flashing character. Each evening Harrington or his assistant would climb to the lantern room to perform the duties of "light up." After preparing the lamp, Harrington would raise the window shades (kept pulled during the day to prevent discoloration of the lens), and the lens would soon glow with a fixed white beam varied every sixty seconds by a five-second, red flash.

The revolving lens ran on ball bearings, and these had to be cleaned and re-oiled weekly. The little metal balls varied in diameter ever so slightly, and keepers were expected to arrange the balls in a perfectly balanced order so that the lens would not lean to one side. A difference of as much as 1/1000 of an inch would cause the lens to operate irregularly. When the balls were removed for cleaning, they were placed in a small, wooden trough in the exact order that they had been removed from the lens race. The balls were individually cleaned, using kerosene, and dried with linen towels. Clock oil was used to prevent the raceways from rusting and to reduce wear. The Lighthouse Service was very specific regarding Trinidad Head's mechanism: exactly four drops of clock oil must be used and the oil must be of the type only obtainable at the Yerba Buena Island Lighthouse Depot.

Keeper Fred Harrington was in the lantern room performing such routine duties during a storm that was decidedly not routine. Harrington wrote in the log:

The storm commenced on December 28, 1914, blowing a gale that night. The gale continued for the whole week and was accompanied by a very heavy sea from the southwest. On the 30th and 31st, the sea increased and at 3 p.m. on the 31st seemed to have reached its height, when it washed a number of times over (93-foot-high) Pilot Rock, a half mile south of the head. At 4:40 p.m., I was in the tower and had just set the lens in operation and turned to wipe the lantern room windows when I observed a sea of unusual height, then about 200 yeards distant, approaching. I watched it as it came in. When it struck the bluff, the jar was very heavy, and the sea shot up the face of the bluff and over it, until the solid sea seemed to me to be on a level with where I stood in the lantern (196 feet above sea

level). Then it commenced to recede and the spray went 25 feet or more higher. The sea itself fell over onto the top of the bluff and struck the tower about on a level with the balcony, making a terrible jar. The whole point between the tower and the bluff was buried in water. The lens immediately stopped revolving and the tower was shivering from the impact for several seconds.

Whether the lens was thrown off level by the jar on the bluff, or the sea striking the tower, I could not say. Either one would have been enough. However, I had it leveled and running in half an hour. About an hour later another sea threw spray up on the level of the bluff, and the constant jars of the heavy sea was much over normal during the night and the whole of the next day. On the 3rd (of January, 1915), the sea moderated to some extent, but a strong southeast wind and high sea continued until the 5th. During the 26 years that I have been stationed here, there has at no time been a sea of any such size as that of the 31st experienced here: but once during that time have I known the spray to come onto the bluff in front of the tower, and but twice have I seen sea or spray go over Pilot Rock. During the prevalence of this storm, about one-third of the old wharf on the east side of the reservation was washed away, the iron rails laid on the balance of it probably being all that kept the rest from going. The lower part of the division fence on the north side was also damaged to some extent, a number of lengths being washed out by the high sea.

Harrington had experienced one of the greatest storm waves in history. The sea had reached a height of two hundred feet.*

Only the fact that the lighthouse is set back from the cliff edge, protected by a large rocky projection just seaward of the light, saved

---

*Rachel Carson, in her book *The Sea Around Us*, calls the Trinidad Head wave one of the most unusual sea actions of all time. Russell Buckmaster, once officer-in-charge at Trinidad Head and a talented writer in his own right, termed it a "tidal wave." Actually, Trinidad Head's wave was a storm wave, not a tidal wave since the latter are of seismic origin. Furthermore, gigantic storm waves are not unknown on the Pacific Coast. Waves reaching well over one hundred feet in height have been reported at Point Bonita during the mid-1950's and in 1967, at St. George Reef in 1952, and at Tillamook Rock, Oregon in 1934, among other years. Although the height of the wave is not given, it is worthy of note that on February 18, 1967, Pine Island, British Columbia, had its fog alarm building and two lesser structures destroyed by a single, huge storm wave. Another British Columbia light station, Egg Island, was completely destroyed in 1948 by a very large storm wave. Only a timely evacuation by the keepers saved their lives.

Keeper Fred L. Harrington was on duty in Trinidad Head lighthouse when it was struck by a wave which reached a height of over 200 feet. Harrington is wearing the distinguished uniform of the United States Lighthouse Service. (Ralph Hunter)

Trinidad Head's bell house and weight tower. The bell hung on the far side of the bell house. This is the last remaining bell house in California. (Humboldt State University Library)

The barn at Trinidad Head, one of but many lesser structures necessary at most light stations. (U.S. Coast Guard)

Harrington and the light itself. The headland, not the tower, absorbed the shock. Ralph Hunter, Harrington's grandson, was standing in front of the dwelling when the great wave struck. He still remembers seeing the lighthouse (and his grandfather) suddenly hidden in a huge wall of solid, green water.

In 1916 Fred Harrington retired after 28 years at the station. He was succeeded by keeper Edward Wilborg. Moving up from first assistant at Lime Point on San Francisco Bay, Wilborg had only been at Trinidad two years when, in 1918, he received recognition from the Lighthouse Service for rescuing a man in a disabled launch.

The 1920's saw a whaling station established adjacent to the lighthouse wharf. The head was an ideal lookout, and as many as twenty-nine whales a week were hauled ashore for processing. Each whaling season saw over one hundred tank cars of whale oil roll out of town on the Northwestern Pacific Railroad. The stench was horrible, and when the whalers ended their operations in 1929, there were few regrets in Trinidad.

During the 1930's steam schooners were still common along the coast. When the steam schooner *Cleone* left Eureka one stormy day in April, 1931, she encountered huge seas approaching Cape Mendocino. The ship was heavily loaded with big bridge timbers, 14 inches square and 30 feet long. By the time Garner Churchill and his crew arrived in their motor lifeboat from the Humboldt Bay Lifeboat Station, there was a sinking ship and a sea full of bridge timbers. Worst, the timbers were heavy on one end and they floated vertically (sailors call them "deadheads"). The heavy seas were washing over the *Cleone*, tearing her deck load loose. As the waves swept through the floating timbers, the deadheads would rise far into the air and then sink below the surface. When the deadheads rebounded, Churchill would remember, they would "jump clear out of the water and then fall over." In order to reach the *Cleone*, Churchill had to maneuver his lifeboat among the deadheads. As he recalls, "If even one had come up under the boat, I'd have been a goner."

Chief Churchill made it through the high seas and the flying deadheads, and all of *Cleone*'s crew were transferred safely to the 36-foot motor lifeboat. Once out of the wreckage, Churchill faced a new problem. The 36-footer was crowded with survivors and she rode low in the water. It would be unsafe to attempt to bring them back across the breaking Humboldt Bay bar. Churchill decided to take the steam schooner's crew to Trinidad and attempt to land them there.

When he arrived at Trinidad, it was so rough that seas were covering the wharf with water and there was no place to dock the motor lifeboat. In an effort to assist bringing the survivors ashore, two local boatmen attempted to reach the lifeboat by rowing a skiff through the

surf. They were quickly swamped. By mid-day a surfman arrived by land from the Humboldt Bay Lifeboat Station. He borrowed another skiff and succeeded in reaching the lifeboat and bringing the *Cleone*'s captain safely to the beach. However, the surf was still high and a second attempt resulted in a capsized skiff. A larger boat was then tried, using two oarsmen. It, too, swamped in the breakers, hurling both men into the water. As the men struggled in the water, Coast Guardsman Robley W. Pomeroy grabbed two live preservers and jumped overboard from the motor lifeboat, swimming to the aid of the two men. He was able to guide the men through the surf to safety on the beach.

Finally, Churchill found a protected beach to the south of the head where the sea was much quieter. Using a skiff, the *Cleone*'s exhausted crew was finally landed. Their day's work done, Churchill and his crew anchored in Trinidad Harbor, boarding a friendly fishing boat for dinner. After 36 hours with no food and little water, even the fisherman's halibut head chowder tasted great.

Trinidad Head still served the fishermen with its oil lamp as late as 1942, when the beacon was finally electrified. The old bell continued to guide the salmon and halibut fishermen back to the harbor until 1947, when it was removed. New compressed-air horns were placed in the bell house, and Coast Guard keepers now dubbed the structure the "fog shack." That same year the old lens was removed, a more modern 375-millimeter, refracting lens taking its place. The Coast Guard now manned the sentinel, and they determined to solve the recurrent problem of water shortages. Periodically, a buoy tender was worked in close to the head and water was pumped ashore to large tanks. It was a spectacular operation involving long hoses and skillful navigation. Finally, in 1960 a pipe was built from the town of Trinidad and the buoy tender calls ended.

By the late 1960's the Coast Guard had razed the lovely, old dwelling. In its place a modern triplex was built to house three Coast Guardsmen and their families. Although automation occurred in the early 1970's, life at the station was little changed. Coast Guard families still lived in the dwelling and the picturesque sentinel continued to serve mariners. With large numbers of small craft using Trinidad Harbor, the light remained an important navigational aid.

The bell house is silent now, but with the years its historic significance has increased. It is now the last bell house in California. In 1948 the town of Trinidad created a small park and, as an expression of their love for the old sentinel, built a cement replica of the lighthouse, in which they mounted the old lens. Beside the monument the bronze fog

Lighthouse tender Madroño *steams into Trinidad Harbor with supplies. C. 1920. (U.S. Coast Guard)*

bell now hangs quietly, awaiting visitors to the park. Perhaps some day the bell can be rehung in the historic bell house.

Those interested in visiting Trinidad Head lighthouse at its spectacular position on the edge of America may want to contact Coast Guard Group Humboldt Bay for permission. The station is only open to visitors by appointment. Standing by the lighthouse, it is not difficult to understand why those who served at Trinidad Head have always considered it a very special part of their lives.

The Cape Carter, *a 95-foot patrol boat, is one of the principal rescue craft on the Redwood Coast. 1968. (U.S. Coast Guard)*

CRESCENT CITY

Crescent City was an isolated little town in the 1850's, surrounded by rugged mountains and unbridged rivers. Stagecoaches used low-tide beaches as transportation routes, and Indians ferried travelers across the rivers in their dugout canoes. Crescent City would dream of a railroad to the outside world, but the link would never be completed. The town's future lay in its harbor, a crescent-shaped, little port bordered on the south by cliffs 500 feet high and framed to the north by the low hills of Point Saint George. To the east rose the redwood forest; and as the trees were felled, the town grew. Crescent City's future depended upon its ability to establish a safe harbor that would provide a reliable sea route to the West Coast lumber market.

The small, rocky bay had both assets and liabilities. On the debit side was the fact that the harbor was open and unprotected from the south. A local southeasterly, called the "kick back" or "back draft," would follow strong northwesterly winds. The kick back would blow with considerable violence from about 9:30 at night until midnight, when it would die out. Worse, there were so many rocks in the harbor that the *Coast Pilot* would write: "The dangers in the cove and approaches are too numerous to mention in detail."

On the positive side, Crescent City harbor was one of but four northern California ports where the larger 19th century lumber ships could load. Well-protected Humboldt Bay was a fine harbor, but the coves at Noyo and Mendocino City were probably not as safe as Crescent City. On a coast offering almost no refuge, even a rocky bay could look quite promising to mariners.

With Crescent City's incorporation in 1854, its citizens immediately set about improving their harbor. The port's leaders approached the California State Legislature for help in obtaining a lighthouse. The Legislature passed a resolution urging the state's Congressman to see that the Federal Government provided Crescent City with a light station. As is still true, California politicians had plenty of clout in Washington, D.C.; and in May, 1855, Congress appropriated $15,000 for the station.

Crescent City's success in Washington almost became too much of a good thing. Initial government proposals provided for a large reservation. So large, in fact, that community leaders could see a major portion of their new town turned into a lighthouse reservation. Crescent City was booming, and it had big plans for the future. Bowing to the city's demands, the extent of the proposed light station was re-

Crescent City lighthouse stands atop a small island. 1934. (U.S. Coast Guard)

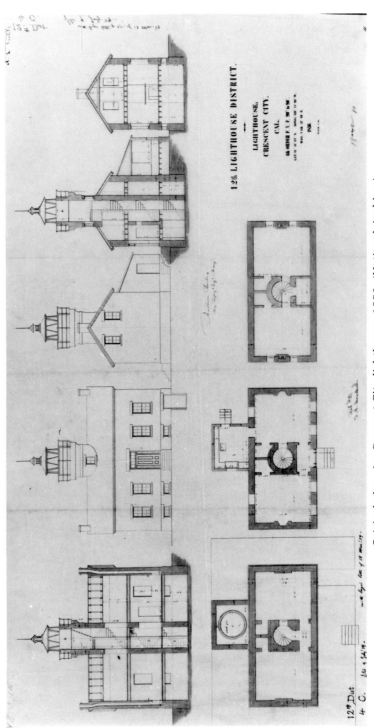

Original plans for Crescent City lighthouse, 1856. (National Archives)

duced to comprise ten acres on Battery Point along with a small, 45-foot-high islet two hundred yards offshore.

The Redwood Coast was still a wild place in 1855. While the Lighthouse Service was busy planning the station, Crescent City was preoccupied with fears that Indians would attack the community. A white man had been killed; and the settlers, always ready to fight the natives, prepared for the worst. When most California Indian "wars" broke out, the "battles" usually consisted of a series of massacres by the whites of any and all nearby Indians. The peaceful Tolowa and Yurok Indians wanted to avoid trouble more than did some of the white vigilante-types, so they came into Crescent City seeking protection. For their own safety, these local Indians were placed on the Battery Point islet until things settled down. Soon, the "enemy" was captured, and three unfortunate Indians were hung at Battery Point.

The following year, the Indians having returned to their homes, the lighthouse work was contracted out, and construction superintendent Potter and his crew began work on the new station. The rock-like islet had been selected as the best site for the beacon. Access was not too difficult because the rock was an island only twice a day. During high tide, the sea surrounded the islet, rendering it inaccessible. During low water, the ocean floor was uncovered and the rock could be reached by strolling across the bottom. Although a boat could land at the island's south end during calm weather, it was easier just to carry materials across during low tide.

As work progressed, a cellar was excavated and a stone foundation laid. The rising sentinel was built in the Lighthouse Service's preferred 1850's style, a short tower surrounded by a Cape Cod cottage. The one-and-a-half-story dwelling portion was of stone, while the 50-foot-high tower was built of brick. The completed beacon had white walls, red roof, green shutters, and a black lantern room. A fourth order lens was installed in the iron lantern room.

On December 10, 1856 everything was ready except the new keeper. Construction superintendent Potter assigned one of his men, Mr. Van Court, to serve as temporary keeper. When they lighted the lamp that night, the lens began showing its distinctive fixed white beam, varied by a bright, white flash once every 90 seconds.

Van Court tended the beacon until keeper Theophilis Magruder arrived on Christmas Day. Magruder found that he was to be keeper of a single-family station with few outbuildings and no fog signal. Situated atop the islet, the sentinel's light was 77 feet above the sea and could be seen for 14 miles.

Theophilis Magruder had come a long way to reach Crescent City. A native of Washington, D.C., his parents had been friends of President James Madison. Magruder had seen gold nuggets displayed in Washing-

Crescent City lighthouse's first keeper, Theophilis Magruder, sitting in a chair made by his old partner, James Marshall. (Del Norte County Historical Society)

Hides Stuart Magruder, wife of station's pioneer keeper, was the first woman to live in the historic lighthouse. Most keepers' wives shared in the responsibility of tending the beacon. (Del Norte County Historical Society)

ton; and the lure of gold fascinated both Magruder and a friend, one James Marshall. Together, they traveled to Oregon in search of gold. Both were unsuccessful, and in 1845 they split up. Magruder and his family remained in the Willamette Valley, while Marshall went to California. It was a fateful decision. James Marshall settled at Coloma, and in 1848 made his world-famous discovery that was to trigger the Gold Rush.

Magruder and his wife, the former Hides Stuart, came to Crescent City to be light keepers. They had no gold, but the new keeper could sit in a chair made by his old partner and reminisce. As he looked out across the sparkling harbor toward the soaring redwoods, perhaps Magruder realized that his choice had not been a bad one either.

Being a Crescent City wickie did not shower anyone with fame, but the keeper certainly received an impressive variety of supplies from the Lighthouse Service. The novice keeper was shipped the necessities of light keeping: two lantern curtains with 12 brass rings (to shield the lens from the sun's rays), rouge and an applicator brush (for polishing the lens), scissors (to trim the wicks), whiting (for making putty), pencils, a hand lantern, soldering iron, brooms, sandpaper, scrub brushes, turpentine, buff skins, paper tripoli, accounting books, and a goodly supply of the triplicate forms the Lighthouse Service wanted completed whenever it shipped such a multitude of items to its isolated employees.

Magruder went about faithfully polishing, cleaning, maintaining, and filling out triplicate forms until, in August, 1859 he received a demoralizing letter from the "Light-House Board," informing him that the pay of all Pacific Coast keepers was being reduced from $1,000 to $600 annually, effective in September. Magruder resigned in November.

A succession of four keepers tended the beacon into the 1870's. During that time the station suffered from the elements. New shingles were required, the staff which supported the lightning rod was blown down and broken, rafters needed to be replaced, floor and rafter timbers became rotten, and the station roadway was destroyed by the sea.

By 1874 conditions had deteriorated so badly that the Lighthouse Service reported to Congress that the station was "dilapidated" and that all of the interior woodwork would have to be removed. It was further suggested that even the existence of the lighthouse was of questionable value. Crescent City harbor was too dangerous to enter at night, it was claimed, and coastwise vessels had to pass so far offshore when rounding St. George Reef that they could not see the light. It was suggested that if a new lighthouse were built on Point St. George, Crescent City light could be abandoned. Eventually, a second light was built, but it was at the northwest extremity of St. George Reef, not on the nearby point. As a consequence, Crescent City remained a necessary and increasingly important navigational aid.

In 1875 John H. Jeffrey became keeper. The first assistant was his wife, Nellie Hamilton Jeffrey. The Jeffreys had come to California from New England, arriving via the Panama route. A Civil War army captain, Jeffrey had had no interest in a career of Indian fighting after the war ended.

Light keeping was to prove more to the Jeffreys' liking. They were to remain at Crescent City for forty years, one of the longest light-keeping tenures in California history. Nellie Jeffrey would be an official, salaried first assistant keeper until 1882, when her position was eliminated in an economy move. However, she (and most of the wives that were to follow her) would always serve as unofficial keeper when her husband was ill or absent. The Jeffreys soon had the station in good condition, even decorating the storm-porch entrance with many lovely house plants. The station once more received excellent inspection reports and its future again became secure.

The Jeffreys found that light keeping on the little island was a constant challenge. Their children could reach school only at low tide and the roadway was frequently washed out. While Crescent City receives more rain than any other port in California, some years even that was not enough to supply the light station's water needs. The roof above the living quarters collected rain water which then drained into a cistern. During a dry year, keepers had to contract with the city to secure water, a problem that would periodically recur until the final days of manned operation.

During wet years, on the other hand, storms could wreak tremendous damage. During the fiercest conditions, waves would actually sweep up over the top of the light. As conditions worsened, storm panels would be locked over the windows and everyone would huddle inside the lighthouse. One of the more memorable storms sheared the chimney off the kitchen roof. A wave then washed down the chimney and into the kitchen, smashing the stove and setting the room on fire. Miraculously, the next wave that swept down the chimney flooded the kitchen and put out the fire.

Not all the problems came from nature. There were people problems, too. Jeffrey was interested in politics and was an active Republican. His partisan activities offended a local Congressman who demanded his removal for "active and offensive partisanship." The Lighthouse Service ordered him to wear his uniform at all times, an action perhaps to be taken figuratively as well as literally. The keeper put on his uniform and continued his high-quality work at the station.

The Lighthouse Service expected the best from its employees. In

Crescent City light has always been exposed to the full fury of the Pacific's storms. Breaking storm wave shoots 75 feet into the air. Larger waves have swept over the top of the lighthouse. (Del Norte County Historical Society)

1887, to make certain that every wickie was faithfully tending his duty, the masters of all steamers were asked to report any lights not functioning properly.

The next year the Lighthouse Service was compelled to issue a far grimmer warning to its workers. A smallpox epidemic had broken out in a number of California ports, and keepers and their families were required to receive vaccinations "without delay." Any smallpox victims were to be immediately removed from the light station, placed in a hospital, and "disinfectants used at once."

When another letter arrived in June, 1889, the Jeffreys may well have expected the worst. The Service informed its personnel that Congress had failed to appropriate adequate funds to pay the keepers. Thus, four per cent of each wickie's salary was to be immediately deducted to cover the difference.

Another continuing "people problem" was the presence of squatters. The Lighthouse Service had made little use of the ten acres on Battery Point. The squatters were both persistent and annoying in their occupancy, so the Lighthouse Service decided to play their own game. The ten acres was subdivided and auctioned off to the squatters. Since they were going to live there anyway, the government might as well earn a few dollars from the reality of the situation.

When the Jeffreys concluded their forty years at Crescent City in 1915, they could look back with pride. Under their charge, the station had always been well run, and they had successfully reared four children despite many obstacles. Their son, George, had followed in his parents' footsteps, becoming keeper of Oakland Harbor lighthouse and rising to be Superintendent of the Buoy Depot on Yerba Buena Island.

The Jeffreys' successor was John E. Lind. When Lind and his wife, Theresa, moved onto the islet, they assumed control of one of the most pleasant stations in California. They certainly deserved it. Lind had spent five years (1887-1892) helping build St. George Reef lighthouse, the most dangerous construction work ever undertaken by the U.S. Lighthouse Service. When the beacon was completed in 1892, Lind stayed on to serve as assistant keeper. Duty at St. George Reef was probably the harshest in the country, and Lind's eight years on the tiny rock must have been difficult ones. After leaving St. George Reef, he rose to be principal keeper at Pigeon Point in San Mateo County. Now he had returned to the Redwood Coast.

The station Lind inherited had changed a bit since its beginnings. In 1907 a new lens had been installed. It was also of the fourth order, but it produced a white flash every 15 seconds. Furthermore, its lamps

The dangers of Crescent City harbor are clearly evident: countless rocks and heavy seas. It is low tide, and the natural causeway connecting the lighthouse island to the mainland is visible at right. February, 1960. (U.S. Coast Guard)

burned kerosene instead of lard oil, and the station could now boast an oil house and a new, 5,000-gallon water tank.

Lind completed his years and was then followed by Jacob Marhoffer. Marhoffer served the station only a short while, resigning to take a job in town. In April, 1925 a giant waterspout was seen twirling across the sea toward Crescent City. As the waterspout reached shore it was transformed into a tornado. The "twister" then proceeded to skip about the town destroying buildings. The Hobbs, Wall store (where Marhoffer often worked) was hit, a theater lost its top story, and then the wind hit the Marhoffer family residence. The tornado demolished a few more buildings, then raced down a railroad track, shoving along piles of lumber and carrying hundreds of board feet into the air. Shaken residents picked through the wreckage as the wind blew itself out near the foothills. It would not be the last time that nature would threaten to destroy Crescent City.

The passage of the 1930's and 1940's saw James Simonsen, Fred Saunders, and John Hollenbeck tending the beacon. Then, in 1946 Wayne Piland and his family arrived. They had been stationed at Yerba Buena Island during World War II. Now they were back on the North Coast.

They soon found Crescent City lighthouse was rich in the intriguing lore of the sea. One of the Pilands' predecessors had claimed that the island was, for a time, visited by miniature mermaids. He reportedly befriended the tiny mermaids and, through food and kindness, managed to entice them up onto the rock and into the lighthouse. It was an interesting yarn, remarkably similar to a Yurok Indian tradition which also describes little creatures visiting the lighthouse rock.

Less fantastic and better documented were the sounds of ghostly footsteps that would climb the tower during very stormy nights. When foul weather approached and during a night of very bad weather, unseen "feet" would slowly climb the stairs with the sound of heavy sea boots. Interestingly, it was during such storms that early light keepers felt their greatest responsibilities and had to repeatedly climb the tower to maintain a close watch over the light. At least six reliable people have heard the "steps" in recent decades.

In any case, Crescent City light's ethereal inhabitants were always friendly and any difficulties the Pilands encountered at their new station were much more concrete. It was winter when they moved into the station. It had been a hard winter, and one of Piland's predecessors had become ill and had to leave the station at the very season when he would normally be doing the most maintenance work. It was Piland's responsibility to return the station to normal.

Heavy rains had left two feet of water in the basement, sloshing among little islands of coal bags and sacks of ruined potatoes. The rain

Wayne R. Piland, one of the Pacific Coast's great light keepers, cleans the lantern room windows at Crescent City lighthouse. After severe storms, Piland could be seen removing seaweed and rocks from the top of the tower. C. 1950. (Wayne Piland Family)

gutters leaked, losing fresh water that was supposed to flow into the cistern to provide the coming summer's water supply. The weather had even managed to penetrate the lantern room. Thus there was water from the top of the beacon to the bottom. Everywhere, in fact, except where it was supposed to be—in the cistern. Storm waves had even swept up over the top of a tall water tank, creating brackish drinking water.

Piland patched, bailed, cleaned, painted, and dried the place out. He covered the top of the water tank with double layers of canvas, nailed the canvas down with large copper tacks, and then shrank the canvas into a water-tight cover using fresh water. Before the canvas had dried, he painted it; and from then on he had a tank cover "as tight as a drum."

Once the maintenance problems were solved, the Pilands began dealing with the challenges of daily life on their semi-island. It was too dangerous to attempt to cross the channel to the mainland by boat during high tide, so all trips to town or school had to be scheduled during low tide. Grocery stores, hardware stores, feed stores, and the like could be visited at any convenient time during the day, but schools required regular hours and attendance. Nature didn't always arrange her tides to coincide with the hours selected by the school board. Despite tide tables reading "low water," the winds sometimes built up such heavy seas that a crossing was impossible even at low tide. The Lighthouse Service had long owned a duplex house on Battery Point as a shore facility for men stationed at St. George Reef lighthouse. No longer used by the offshore keepers, Martha Piland would spend weekdays living there with the two Piland children, Nancy and Donald, during periods when the tides interfered with school schedules or storms made the crossing unsafe. During these times, Wayne Piland lived alone at the lighthouse. With improved weather and favorable tides, Mrs. Piland and the children returned for prolonged stays at home in the lighthouse. During summer vacation, of course, the shore quarters were never used.

Life on the island was good. Although there was not enough spare water for gardening, chickens could be kept, and a large, fenced chicken yard was maintained. Poison oak was a problem for a time, but a pair of goats with voracious appetites eradicated that itchy problem. The goats loved the island and would climb the fences and gambol on the chicken-house roof.

The Pilands particularly enjoyed the fine, old carpenter shop. Here most of the station's repair work was done, and Wayne Piland even built a boat in it. Nearby was the oil house which contained combustible liquids, including oil for the heaters, kerosene, and cleaning fluids.

Winter evenings were spent in the dwelling portion of the lighthouse, often reading. The old log books were a particular pleasure to read. The Pilands also enjoyed the old Lighthouse Service "doctor book," which prescribed what medicines keepers should select from the medicine chest supplied by the Lighthouse Service. Each set of symptoms was numbered and had a corresponding cure, often a mixture containing a heavy dose of opium. As the Pilands sat reading, they were warmed by their cookstove's coal fire. Their home was now lighted by electricity; and trucks, instead of horses and wagons, delivered supplies.

In the winter of 1950 a great storm swept into Del Norte County, the worst Piland would experience in a lifetime of light keeping. High winds and huge waves developed very quickly, and the day turned dark gray. On the mainland, motorists attempting to reach Crescent City from the south on U.S. Highway 101 soon found themselves in a terrifying situation as 300-foot-high redwood trees began falling across the road. Electrical power was lost almost immediately, and lanterns flickered in the rooms at the waterfront's old Surf Hotel. From the hotel lobby's windows it was possible to see the harbor. No one wanted to stand close to the rattling windows for fear they would blow in, but it was soon clear that the harbor was taking a terrible beating. The new jetty was nearing completion, built of stones, some so large that big dump trucks could only carry one at a time. The storm had halted work, and as conditions worsened, the sea began tearing the jetty apart. Huge stones were washed away and large gaps appeared in the jetty. Boats started to drag anchor, washing ashore. A barge was loosened and began to batter a dock to pieces. Another, larger barge held a massive contruction crane. It, too, had been torn loose from its moorings, and it was pounded by seas that broke high in the air. Soon it was driven ashore, going up far onto the beach.

Crescent City lighthouse stood outside the jetty, at the most exposed location in the harbor. Huge waves began washing up and over the lighthouse. Inside the lighthouse, behind heavy boarded panels swung into place and securely latched over the dwelling windows, the Pilands maintained a 24-hour watch. Often, they thought that the next wave would smash the panels and burst into their home. During intermittent periods of improved visibility, Piland took his binoculars and his "long glass" and "maintained a mother's watch" over the harbor and the jetty. Both were disintegrating in the storm. Piland took hourly barometric readings, and on the second day conditions appeared to be improving. Spray was no longer hitting the side of the lighthouse, and it finally seemed safe to venture outdoors. Piland began to ease out the back door. He didn't get far. Suddenly, a great wave of solid green water hit him right in the face, knocking him over.

By the third day, the storm had passed. Keeper Piland made a careful inspection of the station. The sea had carried gravel from the ocean floor up into the rain gutters on the lighthouse roof. Piland also discovered seaweed hanging from the roof, over seventy feet above normal water. Most of the station's fresh-water supply had been ruined by sea water washing off the roof, down the gutters, and into the cistern.

Piland went down to Citizen's Dock and used a radio on a commercial fishing boat to call Coast Guard headquarters on Humboldt Bay to inform them of the damage. He reported that windows high in the lantern room had been cracked by the gigantic seas and the tower had taken on quite a bit of water, but that the light was operable and had not failed. He did not report that the mysterious, heavy steps of the Crescent City lighthouse ghost had climbed the tower each hour on the hour.

Mr. Piland leaded in the cracked lantern room windowpanes and later replaced the broken windows. Crescent City light had withstood one of its most severe challenges. Seas had reached a height of at least

85 feet and undoubtedly had, at times, surpassed 100 feet in height.

Lesser storms had presented problems too. When Piland first came to Crescent City, it was not uncommon to see fishing boats driven ashore by southerly storms. During rough weather, the low-water crossing to the mainland could be treacherous. Piland would watch the ocean to see if it was "building up" to rush in and flood the causeway. Once, three Coast Guard officers over-stayed their visit during an inspection. Piland warned them that the tide was rising and the sea building up. The officers, however, were bent on a thorough inspection. Finally satisfied, they attempted the crossing, since the causeway still appeared to be dry. Part-way across, a large wave came sneaking in, rising up about the men, thoroughly drenching them and nearly forcing them to swim for shore.

Piland himself was caught once. It was necessary to take his daughter across during heavy weather. The ocean had pulled back and the crossing appeared safe. Together, father and daughter picked their way across the rocky bottom. Suddenly a big buildup occurred and seas swept across the causeway. Piland boosted Nancy atop a rock. Then both of them clung to the boulder as the sea rushed by. Nancy credits her father's quick thinking with saving their lives.

All of Crescent City's keepers dreaded the possibility of a high-water crossing. During the Coast Guard years, the station was equipped with a one-man, rubber life raft, used mainly for pleasure boating on calm days. It was the only possible link to the mainland if emergencies occurred during high water.

One cold night, the Pilands had been entertaining overnight guests, an elderly couple who enjoyed visiting the station. About 11 p.m. the wife slipped and fell, painfully breaking both wrists. She needed immediate medical attention, but the tide was in. After much telephoning, Piland found a doctor willing to risk the crossing. Fortunately, sea conditions were calm and there was no swell.

Piland rowed across the channel in his one-man raft and met the doctor on Battery Point. The raft was too small to accommodate two adults. For maximum stability, Piland had the doctor lie down in the raft, a proposition that held little appeal for the medical man. However, the dedicated physician finally became convinced of Piland's judgment and lay down on the bottom of the raft. Piland then entered the water, pulling the raft along with him. Soon the water was up to the keeper's shoulders and his feet could not touch bottom. The raft began leaking, filling halfway with water. Light keeper and doctor finally made the crossing, albeit both were very cold and wet when they arrived at the island.

Once at the station, using shingles obtained from the carpenter shop, the doctor set the woman's wrists. Then, well past midnight,

Interior of old Crescent City lighthouse lens showing oil lamp along with "bull's eye" and prisms of a flash panel. (R. Shanks)

Piland returned the doctor to the mainland, once again using the life-raft. The dripping medical man bid the light keeper farewell, and Piland rowed back to tend the light.

The Piland family continued to tend Crescent City lighthouse until October, 1953, when it was automated. That month the station's last inspection occurred, with inspector C. W. Harwood declaring the light-house to be "in an outstanding condition of cleanliness and mainte-nance." Soon afterward the buoy tender *Magnolia* arrived, tying up at Citizen's Dock. The crew from the tender came to the light station to assist the Pilands in moving. The crew formed a human chain and passed the family's boxed belongings down the island, across the sea floor, and up Battery Point into a truck. The truck (which was nor-mally used to haul St. George Reef supplies down to the dock) carried the family possessions to the *Magnolia*. The tender then steamed south, bound for the Pilands' last assignment, another tour of duty at Yerba Buena Island Light Station.

The old Crescent City lens was removed during conversion to auto-matic operation. A more modern 375-millimeter lens became the senti-nel's third and final lens. The historic station was then leased by the

Today, Crescent City remains one of the best preserved and most historic of America's lighthouses. Notice the massive stone walls of the dwelling area. 1976. (R. Shanks)

Coast Guard to the Del Norte County Historical Society as a museum.

Historical Society curators continued to live in the lighthouse after the Pilands left. During this period, the lighthouse again faced a challenge from the sea. The 1964 Alaskan earthquake triggered massive seismic waves, and tidal wave warnings were broadcast along the northern California coast. About midnight on March 27, four waves hit Crescent City with tremendous force, sweeping far inland and destroying most of the city's commercial area, the harbor, and many homes. Eleven people were dead or missing. Fires and explosions followed as the last waves receded. As the 95-foot Coast Guard cutter *Cape Carter* returned to aid in rescue operations, it sighted the Coast Guard building from Citizen's Dock floating in the sea. The building was taken in tow, much like a disabled vessel.

Amid the terrible devastation, Crescent City lighthouse stood firm, its rock-solid island base and two-foot-thick walls withstanding one of the most powerful waves ever to strike our coast.

Today, the ancient beacon may still be visited during low tide. A new automatic beacon at the tip of the jetty has replaced the lighthouse as a functioning navigational aid, but the old sentinel is virtually unchanged since the time of the Pilands—or, for that matter, the days of the Magruders and Jeffreys. The entire station is preserved and may be toured. The original banjo clock still hangs from the wall, and the old guest register is still to be seen. The lighthouse is the pride of Crescent City, the finest example of the 1850's lighthouse architecture in all of northern California.

ST. GEORGE REEF

Among hundreds of American lighthouses, three sentinels stand out as unparalleled engineering accomplishments: Minot's Ledge in Massachusetts; Tillamook Rock in Oregon; and St. George Reef in California. All three were built on wave-swept rocks at stormy, dangerous locations. Of the three, St. George Reef is the tallest and largest. It cost more and took longer to build, and it has proven more dangerous to those who manned it than either Minot's or Tillamook. St. George Reef is undoubtedly the greatest lighthouse in America.

Barely three miles north of Crescent City is a low, hilly point, sandy and almost treeless. Traditional home of the Tolowa Indians, in 1792 British explorer George Vancouver named the promontory "Point St. George" in honor of England's patron saint. Beyond the point, Vancouver sighted a reef, extending seaward for six miles. The reef was composed of nine visible rocks and many sunken ledges. With a mixture of English humor and mariner's caution, Vancouver dubbed them the "Dragon Rocks."

The name was well chosen, and it is still occasionally used by light keepers and commercial fishermen. But the term "Dragon Rocks" has largely been dropped from official usage, and the reef now bears the same name as the point. The beastly character of the reef remains, however; and the *Pacific Coast Pilot* warns:

All the rocks of St. George Reef rise abruptly (and) when in the vicinity, soundings give no warning of their presence. In thick weather the greatest caution should be observed and the reef given wide berth.

The first lighthouse in the area was built at Crescent City in 1856. The new beacon was a helpful harbor light and was of some use to vessels approaching from the south. However, Crescent City light was a dozen miles from the reef's outermost rocks, and from the north was completely hidden by the hills of Point St. George. The delay in establishing a light station on St. George Reef was to mean that Crescent City would come to have a cemetery filled with shipwreck victims.

On July 28, 1865, the passenger steamer *Brother Jonathan* left San Francisco bound for the Pacific Northwest. The ship's owners had so criminally overloaded the *Brother Jonathan* with both passengers and cargo that the captain refused to take command of the ship. Finally, under threat of dismissal, the master reluctantly gave in to the owners, and the jammed ship steamed out of San Francisco Bay. As she pro-

St. George Reef, America's greatest lighthouse. (Steven Yarbrough)

ceeded up the coast, the *Brother Jonathan* encountered increasingly severe head winds and seas. Passing Crescent City, she fired the routine one-gun salute. North of Point St. George, however, the weather worsened, and the overloaded vessel could no longer make headway. The endangered ship came about and attempted to reach the harbor at Crescent City, although to do so required passing through St. George Reef. During heavy weather St. George Reef "smokes" (produces thick, smoke-like spray), and the rocks can become completely obscured. Lacking seamarks, the position of the reef is almost impossible to judge. As the *Brother Jonathan* passed through the reef, she struck the reef with great force, ripping her bottom out. It was Sunday, July 30, just ten minutes before two o'clock in the afternoon.

There was little that could be done. The Indians at Point St. George had heard a cannon firing distress signals. Then, at about five p.m. a small, crowded lifeboat was seen rounding Crescent City lighthouse. Its 19 occupants were the wreck's only survivors. Accounts vary, but at least 166 persons drowned in what remains as California's worst shipwreck.

The need for a light and fog signal on St. George Reef had been tragically established. By 1866-67, the Lighthouse Board requested that the area be reserved for lighthouse purposes; but the site was so remote and so dangerous that it would be fifteen years before Congress would fund construction of a lighthouse on Northwest Seal Rock, the most exposed portion of the reef.

Oregon's Tillamook Rock lighthouse had been completed in 1881, a feat which gained construction superintendent A. Ballantyne worldwide acclaim among lighthouse authorities. His experience at Tillamook Rock and his acquaintance with skilled workmen willing to accept the risks of such work made Ballantyne an ideal choice to direct construction at St. George Reef.

Guided by a group of sea-lion hunters familiar with the reef, Ballantyne and some of his best workmen first landed on wave-swept Northwest Seal Rock in 1882 to begin survey work. Before the survey could be completed, however, large seas drove the men from the rock. During the coming month, landing was to prove so difficult that Ballantyne was able to return on only three occasions. As winter approached, the weather worsened and all further work was suspended.

In April, 1883, after a rough voyage during which his ships were forced to turn back twice, Ballantyne returned to the reef, only to find the sea breaking over the top of the 54-foot-high rock. Ballantyne was on board the wrecking steamer *Whitelaw*, which had another vessel, the *La Ninfa*, under tow. A former sealing schooner, the *La Ninfa* had most recently been used as a makeshift lightship marking a wreck off San Francisco. As it would be impossible to establish a work camp on the

Late stages of construction at St. George Reef lighthouse. 1891. (U.S. Coast Guard)

rock itself, the *La Ninfa* would be permanently moored nearby as a barracks ship. A single mooring buoy was established and the *La Ninfa* secured to it. Before the remaining mooring buoys could be placed, a storm arose and the crew retreated to the steamer, leaving the tenuously anchored schooner unmanned.

The *Whitelaw* spent an entire week riding out the storm. Miraculously, the *La Ninfa*'s single mooring held, although the builders were soon to encounter new difficulties. Taking soundings preparatory to placing the remaining mooring buoys, Ballantyne was stunned to find the ocean was far deeper than had been reported when a lighthouse tender had conducted soundings in 1881. There was nothing to do but steam back to Humboldt Bay for longer chains and larger buoys.

While the *Whitelaw* was in port, another storm blew in. Ballantyne hurried back to St. George Reef only to find the *La Ninfa* gone. The *Whitelaw* spent nearly a week hunting for the schooner, finally returning in discouragement to Humboldt Bay to refuel. The crewless schooner was still afloat, however, drifting up and down the Redwood Coast. She had even weathered a gale off Cape Mendocino without benefit of a single human hand. Encouraged by a reported sighting, the *Whitelaw* shoved off again and by good fortune found the ship drifting between Trinidad Head and Crescent City.

Taking the *La Ninfa* under tow, the long-suffering crew arrived back at the reef on May 6, 1883. Ballantyne was elated by the scene there— the sea was so calm it resembled a lake.

Ballantyne was not about to have the *La Ninfa* drift away again. The barracks ship was anchored using four mooring buoys held in place by sinkers weighing from 8,000 to 12,000 pounds. No less than three large anchors were placed as an added precaution.

Fair weather lasted just long enough to land on the reef, drive ring bolts into the rock, run lines, and land a donkey engine. With everything in place the *Whitelaw* could be allowed to leave. Supplies and mail would arrive once every ten days on the steam schooner *Crescent City*. Light keeper Jeffrey at his post at Crescent City light was asked to make progress reports to the Lighthouse Service each time a ship returned from the reef.

The *La Ninfa* was moored 350 feet off Northwest Seal Rock. A surfboat was rowed across the choppy water to land workers on the reef. With strong currents, rough seas, and very cold water, it was a slow and dangerous commute. With each swell the surfboat rose and fell, making it risky to leap from the boat to the slippery rock. Once there, the rock offered no shelter.

The first task was to carve a base for the lighthouse foundation. Northwest Seal Rock had always been a wave-washed rock, and re-

Engine room in the base of St. George Reef lighthouse. C. 1920. (U.S. Coast Guard)

ducing its height to provide room for a foundation would only compound the problem. A means of quickly evacuating the rock would have to be devised or the workers would be in constant peril.

Ballantyne devised an aerial tramway that would lessen the danger. He had 2½-inch wire rope run from a ring bolt atop the rock down through the La Ninfa's masts to a spar buoy moored beyond the ship. The wire rope was rigged so that it could be taut as the La Ninfa rolled. A circular, box-like "cage" was hung from a block that ran on the wire rope. The donkey engine was used to pull the cage up to the rock, carrying either men or materials. The cage was only four feet in diameter, but as many as five or six workers could ride it at one time.

The cage was most useful when the sea built up and it became necessary to flee the reef. Ballantyne constantly watched the ocean, his experience at Tillamook giving him an uncanny ability to predict when a swell would break over the rock. At Ballantyne's warning shout, the workers would tie their tools to ring bolts and make a dash for the "flying cage." Gravity carried the cage swiftly down to the schooner. Quick use of the donkey engine would have the cage back on the rock in three minutes. With luck, Ballantyne could evacuate two or three dozen men in twenty minutes.

As their confidence in the cage increased, some of the men would continue working until the sea was surging over the entire work area. Then, at the last possible moment, they would climb into the flying cage and roll down to the La Ninfa. (The wire rope parted once, but fortunately the cage was still over the rock and no one drowned when the cage fell.)

A great excavation, shaped much like an inverted pyramid, had to be blasted in the rock to hold the lighthouse. The explosives used were a glycerine powder. The powder was of necessity stored on the rock itself and fear of an accidental explosion added to the strain of the project. In an attempt to protect the glycerine, a hole was cut in the rock's summit and a magazine built of heavy timbers. Inside, the powder was carefully wrapped in many layers of canvas. Each time a large sea broke over the rock and battered the magazine around under its four-inch rope netting, there was the terrible threat of an explosion.

The glycerine powder was necessary because the rock was extremely hard. It was also brittle. When blasting was in progress, the brittle stone shot high in the air showering the men with rocks. Ballantyne recalled that the workers "had to hunt their holes like crabs" to avoid being hit. Even the La Ninfa was pelted and her bulwarks and barracks smashed, although no serious damage was done to the schooner "save her appearance."

By late September, 1883, the excavation was completed and the site ready for the lighthouse. However, an unexpected comber swept

Original steam fog whistles mounted atop the lighthouse base. Note large pile of sacks of newly arrived coal at right. C. 1911. (U.S. Coast Guard)

These vertical mushroom fog horns replaced the original steam fog horns. C. 1920. (U.S. Coast Guard)

the rock, knocking two quarrymen thirty feet down the rock, where, badly cut and bruised, they barely managed to avoid drowning. After that, the men and tools were returned to the *La Ninfa.* On October 2 the *Crescent City* arrived to transport most of the workmen to San Francisco. The *La Ninfa* left under sail. The work crew was laid off for the winter, and the tools were stored at the Yerba Buena Island Lighthouse Depot.

During the fall, preparations were made to build a wharf, workmen's quarters, and a stonecutter's shed on Humboldt Bay's North Spit (just north of the lifesaving station). While in Humboldt County, Ballantyne was approached by the contractor, a Mr. Simpson, who reported the discovery of granite nearby on the Mad River. The stone proved to be of high quality and a quarry was established. The Mad River and Arcata Railroad began deliveries during the spring of 1884.

The Mad River quarry was to yield all of the 1,339 granite blocks needed. With inadequate Congressional appropriations, the years 1884-86 saw most work limited to the shore. By 1887, additional funding had added new life to the project. Unfortunately, just as Congress loosened its purse strings, nature unleashed its storms. Winter rains washed down immense mud slides at the quarry. The mud engulfed railroad tracks, derricks, and partially cut stone. A short distance away stood the main pile of undressed stone, about 1,500 pieces awaiting shipment to the North Spit. Suddenly, the entire pile gave way, slid down a hill, and embedded itself in soft soil at the foot of the hill.

The North Spit wharf had been having its problems, too. Teredos, marine shipworms similar to termites, had completely destroyed the piles that supported the wharf. Work had to be concentrated, not at the lighthouse site, but at the quarry and the wharf. It took two months' labor just to recover from winter. The delays also forced the chartering of three new ships.

The steamers *Santa Maria* and *Alliance* were contracted to transport men, equipment, stones, and other supplies to the reef. The schooner *Sparrow* would serve as the barracks ship. Ballantyne found St. George Reef's summer as troublesome as Humboldt Bay's winters: "The season (1887) was remarkable for the prevalence of strong northwest winds, the whole summer being a succession of heavy gales, making construction difficult and dangerous. . . ." Storms had cracked the boom of the derrick used to hoist the cut stone onto the rock, but it was eventually repaired and four additional booms set up. Soon, cut stones averaging two and a half tons each were being hoisted onto the rock. The stones were dovetailed so that all interlocked with one another on each side and above and below. Reportedly, each had been carefully prefitted with its mates at the North Spit stoneyard prior to being shipped to the reef.

At times, even such huge stones were no match for the Pacific. During a June gale, a 7,000-pound stone was torn from its bed and thrown to a higher level of the foundation. Fortunately, the crew had already evacuated the rock due to heavy sea conditions, and no one was hurt.

Despite all, at the close of the season's work in October, 1887, the lighthouse base had risen 22 feet. That winter much of the remaining quarry and stone work was completed.

The 1888 season was short, but productive. Using the *Whitelaw* and the steam schooner *Del Norte*, the lighthouse rose to 32 feet in height. Significantly, the tower was now tall enough so that workmen's quarters could be constructed on the rock, saving much time and effort otherwise lost in getting on and off the reef.

Then winter's seas prevented months of work. It was not until April, 1889, that the *Del Norte* left Humboldt Bay to begin another season. Arriving at the reef with a work force of fifty men, the workmen's quarters, built of heavy timbers, were found to have been badly damaged by winter storms. The quarters were repaired, but not for long. At two o'clock one May morning a gigantic sea hit the rock, washing men from their bunks and smashing the quarters. No one was injured, but the destruction continued to slow progress. When work ended in October, eight more courses had been completed, for a total of twenty-one courses. The lower tower, with its boiler room, coal rooms, and storage room, had been built up and arched over.

Lack of funding meant virtually no progress during the year 1890. However, the next year proved quite different. The year 1891 saw Ballantyne using still another ship, the steam schooner *Sunol*. By April 17, the *Sunol* was jammed with fifty workmen and a cargo of stone, sand, cement, derricks, moorings, lumber, rope, tackle, and fresh water. Everything sat at the wharf for four days until the Humboldt Bay bar was calm enough to risk a crossing. Then it was off to the rock. Arriving at St. George Reef, Ballantyne "found our quarters on the rock badly wrecked and no mooring buoys in sight." April and May were rainy with strong southerly winds and heavy seas; but from May through September the weather was favorable.

After spending two weeks repairing storm damage, work began to progress rapidly. The tower was rising. Each stone had been precisely cut so that no more than 3/16-inch clearance was allowed. Between layers of stone two-inch gun-metal dowels helped secure the stones to one another. Cement and cut stone were forced in to fill even the smallest separation. In a short while, the large, caisson-like base rose to its full 70 feet in height; and except for its passageways, rooms, and a 120,000-gallon cistern, it was filled with reinforced concrete. Above the base, the light tower grew in stature as scaffolding soared over one

Most dangerous aspect of life on St. George Reef was getting on and off the light station. Small boats such as this one were always used. C. 1935. (U.S. Coast Guard)

hundred feet above the sea. Hoists and derricks carried stones and mortar up the tower, using steam winches for power.

In the midst of the final stages of construction, tragedy struck. A rigger, while letting go of one of the tag lines on the big derrick's boom, was carried over the pier and killed. This was the only death incurred during construction. St. George Reef's light keepers would come to pay a much higher toll.

In order to finish the project, work was continued well into October. By that time everything was completed except installation of the lens which had yet to arrive from France. But it was now late in the season and the sea conditions had become increasingly bad. Ballantyne found that, although the sentinel was virtually completed, due to heavy seas he could not get his workers off the lighthouse. It was November 8 before his men dared to leave the lighthouse for the waiting steamer. Finally, men and tools were safely on board the *Sunol*, the moorings were lifted, and the ship sailed for Yerba Buena Island Lighthouse Depot. Three of the workmen had been appointed keepers; and although they did not yet have a light, they remained on St. George Reef to care for the station.

The completed lighthouse was the tallest on the Pacific Coast of North America, 134 feet in height. Costing $704,000, St. George Reef had become the most expensive lighthouse ever built. The amount was an incredible sum for a nineteenth century lighthouse. The cost was nearly double that of Minot's Ledge and almost five times that of Tillamook Rock. The massive structure had consumed 175,260 cubic feet of granite. The ships had carried 14,307 tons of stone, 1,439 tons of sand, 335 tons of brick, and 272 tons of gravel out to the reef to be used in construction. Interior work had been finished using such fine woods as Port Orford cedar, redwood, and oak. The entire project—from soundings to lighting the lens—had required eleven years, the most prolonged construction period in American lighthouse history.

The lower portion of the lighthouse consisted of an oval base 70 feet high and 68 feet long. At the foot of the base was a concrete landing, equipped with a derrick. From the landing, a stairway led far up the side of the base to an entrance door. The door opened into the engine room, location of the machinery used to power the station's twin, 12-inch steam fog whistles. The whistles protruded from the top of the base, an area which served as the catch basin for the cisterns which were located below the engine room. The base also held a storeroom filled with enough supplies to last the keepers for many months.

The pyramidal tower rose from the easterly end of the base. The tower was square, except for one side where an interior circular stairway was located. As a keeper ascended the tower, he passed first through the boiler, coal and laundry rooms, and then, on each successive level, to the galley, the head keeper's quarters, the assistant keepers' quarters, the watch room (later used as a radio room), and finally into the lantern room. Standing six and a half miles offshore, the magnificent, gray-white tower with its black lantern room stood ready to receive its new lens. It was not until July, 1892, that the lens arrived in San Francisco.

Soon forwarded to the reef, the beautiful first order lens had cost the Lighthouse Service $15,000. It featured plates of red glass covering alternating panels of prisms and bull's eyes which produced an alternating red and white flash with a 15-second interval between flashes. (Later, the red glass plates would be removed, producing a white-only flash.) Beams from the lens warned mariners of the reef any time that they approached within 18 miles of the light.

On October 20, 1892, both the light and fog whistle began operation. Appropriately, much of the lighthouse staff, including head keeper John Olsen and assistant keeper John E. Lind, had helped build the sentinel. They were aided by three other wickies. Due to cramped quarters and an extremely dangerous location, no families would ever be allowed to live at the station. Among all of America's sentinels,

Commissioner of Lighthouses George R. Putnam believed that only two—St. George Reef and Tillamook Rock—were so difficult to operate that they warranted five keepers.

The only means of landing on or leaving St. George Reef light was with the use of a derrick. Heavy seas precluded building a wharf or landing a boat. Any vessel would have to stay a respectable distance from Northwest Seal Rock while transferring personnel or delivering supplies. A 60-foot-long boom had to be lowered to a horizontal position, providing its maximum reach over the water. A hook was then run out to the end of the boom and lowered. A small boat would carefully work its way in under the hook. Nets or cargo bags full of supplies would be attached to the hook and hauled up to the lighthouse. This required split-second timing on the part of the derrick operator at the lighthouse and superb seamanship from those in the boat.

Landing personnel was even more difficult. Using special lines that attached to the boat, the boat and all its occupants would be lifted up and swung onto the rock. Since the sea might be rising and falling as much as fifteen feet while keepers were attempting to attach the boat to the hook, the possibility of capsizing was very real. The water was quite cold at the reef, the current swift, and likelihood of rescue minimal. The station boat was nothing more than an 18-foot sailboat.

Often, waves would be rising and falling fifteen or more feet as keepers attempted to leave the reef. C. 1950. (U.S. Coast Guard)

Much of the time the weather was so bad that the men could not leave the rock anyway. Northwest Seal Rock was frequently awash with heavy swells and it was twelve lonely and dangerous miles through the reef and down the coast to Crescent City. The quarterly calls by lighthouse tender did little more than provide the minimum supplies necessary for survival and to bring the fuel to keep the navigational aids operating.

Life was incredibly hard on the reef station. On October 14, 1893, assistant keeper William Erickson set out from the lighthouse in the little sailboat, bound for Crescent City. Somewhere between the light and the lumber port his sailboat sank and Erickson drowned. In April, 1901, while attempting to hoist another boat from the water, assistant keeper Goffried Olsen broke his leg and had to be transferred to shore duty. In November, 1902, assistant keeper Julius Charter died in Crescent City. At the end of April, 1903, wickie Charles Steiner left St. George Reef seriously ill. By 1918 three more keepers had resigned, two were fired, and another evacuated because of illness. Among the 80 men who would serve the lighthouse from 1891 through 1930, 37 would resign and 26 would seek transfers to other stations.

On the other hand, fearless old John Olsen withstood the harsh life for twenty-two years while he was head keeper. He had once spent seventeen hours in an open boat trying to reach Crescent City. A gasoline launch eventually replaced the station's sailboat; but in 1903 the launch's engine failed during a supply run, and one of Olsen's assistants spent 56 hours aboard the helpless boat "undergoing a perilous experience." The Crescent City light keepers kept a constant watch for the St. George boat and were always ready to go to her assistance, but the trip was long and a man was largely on his own.

Most changes during these years were comparatively minor. A derrick was built at Crescent City to lift the launch from the water. The lighthouse boom was extended out from 60 to 90 feet in length so as "to reach beyond a dangerous eddy just off the rock" that had been the cause of Goffried Olsen's accident in 1901. The blacksmith shop, built at an exposed site along the lighthouse base, was completely wrecked by storm waves and had to be rebuilt.

Passing steamers took pity on the isolated light keepers. The mariners would enclose magazines and newspapers in coal-oil cans and throw them overboard, so that the wickies could lower their boat and retrieve the latest news.

This was a pleasant pastime during fair weather, but sometimes conditions were so fierce that it was impossible even to step outside the tower. In 1923 storm waves reached up seventy feet, swept over the lighthouse base, and tore a donkey engine and its housing from their foundation. During such conditions it was impossible to reach shore, and the reactions of the attendants could take interesting twists.

After John Olsen retired in 1913, John Luckman served as head keeper until 1918. Then George Roux became head keeper. A former sailor of French ancestry, Roux was to remain on the reef for over two decades. In 1937 he and his men experienced some of the harshest weather in St. George Reef's history. Hurricane-force winds and giant seas cut off all contact with the shore. Expected liberty days, mail, fresh supplies all failed to materialize week after week as the storm continued. After a month passed, the wickies began to wonder if they might starve to death. The men had worked together harmoniously for years, but the feeling of being trapped began to change their relations. Disappointment turned to frustration, fear, and even rage. After four weeks, the crew ceased speaking to one another. Meals were eaten in near silence. Just to say "Please pass the salt" became a serious personal affront. The keepers began going to great lengths to ignore each other, especially as the storm roared on into seven weeks. Meals were eaten cold with the men facing away from one another. As George Roux explained, they "were just so fed up with each other's company that it was almost unbearable." Finally, after fifty-nine days of foul weather and isolation, the sixtieth day dawned clear and calm.

Shore quarters for St. George Reef keepers and their families were maintained on Crescent City's Battery Point. Crescent City lighthouse keepers' families also used this house when high tides blocked the access road. 1937. (U.S. Coast Guard)

A supply ship dashed out, bringing boxes and sacks of food as well as a crew of relief keepers. The diet of hardtack and salted pork and beef was over. The incessant blasts of the diaphone fog horns finally stilled. As the weather normalized, so did the relations of the men. Roux recalled that, with the arrival of the supply ship, tension immediately faded. "We were friends again. Talked our heads off," he said.

The inaccessibility of the light station, even in good weather, meant few visitors. From the opening of the station through the termination of Lighthouse Service control in 1939, St. George Reef had an average of just five visitors a year, a figure that included inspectors and lighthouse tender crewmen. Crescent City wickie George Jeffrey had been the first visitor. Theresa Lind, wife of former keeper John Lind, was one of a number of women to brave a visit.

Families lived either in the two small houses the Lighthouse Service maintained on Battery Point in Crescent City or provided their own residences. After World War II, the Coast Guard assumed control of a former Navy radio compass station on Point St. George for use as the St. George Reef Shore Quarters.

The St. George Reef launch landed at the Hobbs, Walls lumber dock in Crescent City when keepers came ashore several times a month. The dock was convenient to Crescent City lighthouse and nearby stores, and featured a good hoist. Occasionally, buoy tenders would tie up here.

During the 1940's, the St. George Reef crew would use the shortwave radio at Crescent City lighthouse to call the reef to learn whether sea conditions would allow them to return to the station. Often the conditions at the reef were entirely different than at Crescent City. Sometimes the weather would take a turn for the worse just as the relief boat left the harbor.

Even being near Crescent City was no guarantee of safety. In November, 1946, the St. George Reef launch was thrown onto the harbor's beach and heavily pounded by breakers until it could be pulled off by an amphibious vehicle. On another occasion Crescent City keeper Wayne Piland and his son, Donald, spotted the St. George Reef boat adrift off Battery Point. Using a commercial fishing boat, the Pilands rushed to the aid of the St. George Reef keepers. A little gasoline worked wonders for the launch's engine.

By the late 1940's Coast Guardsmen had completely replaced civilian keepers at St. George Reef. The Coast Guard continued the Lighthouse Service practice of using a small power boat to reach Crescent City. The 1950's were to be among the harshest years St. George Reef had ever seen. Continued use of the launch was to result in the worst lighthouse tragedy in California history.

On April 5, 1951, the St. George Reef crew was preparing their boat for the wet, choppy run into Crescent City. Coast Guard technicians Bertram Beckett and Clarence Walker had to be taken ashore after completing some electrical work. It was an amiable day, and one of the crew even took some pictures.

By mid-afternoon the three-man boat crew had everything in readiness, their boat prepared to be swung out on the derrick boom and lowered to the water far below. Stanley Costello was at the boat's wheel. Ross Vandenberg was astride the cabin, standing by to unhook the launch once it touched the sea. A third keeper, Thomas Mulcahy, was astern handling a mooring line. After a short wait, Beckett and Walker climbed in. With all five men on board, St. George Reef's officer-in-charge Fred Permenter carefully watched the ocean's swells and then skillfully lowered the boat away. The boat hit the water in the trough of two waves.

Suddenly, a huge swell blasted the launch toward the reef. A second later, the wave's backlash rose up and over the men. An avalanche of water crashed down on them, swamping the boat and throwing everyone into the water.

Despite life jackets, the men were in grave danger. The frigid water and swift currents would soon take their toll; and the station's only boat was now lost. Officer-in-charge Permenter reacted instantly. After sending a desperate distress call to the Humboldt Bay Coast Guard Station, Permenter began an incredible rescue attempt. With his men struggling in the water below, Permenter could see that the only hope of rescue lay with the launch's life raft. The empty, drifting raft must somehow be positioned nearer the lighthouse. After two unsuccessful attempts, Permenter managed to retrieve the life raft. He then climbed down to the foot of the light tower and jumped twenty feet into the sea.

Climbing into the raft, Permenter first went after the two men he had seen drifting away. Fortunately, both had managed to grab hold of the mooring buoy nearby and were now clinging to it. Satisfied that they were momentarily safe, Permenter went after the other three men. Finding one man alive but unconscious, Permenter managed to pull him into the raft. Now nearly exhausted, Permenter worked the raft toward a fourth man. He was dead. Too exhausted to pull the dead Coast Guardsman on board, the officer-in-charge lashed him to the raft. With the additional weight of two men, the raft could no longer be paddled and attempts to locate the fifth keeper failed.

With no Coast Guard rescue boat closer than Humboldt Bay, Group Commander Einar H. Nilson called Wayne Piland at Crescent City light, asking for his help. Piland, accompanied by his son, Donald, who was home on leave from the Navy, immediately went down to Citizen's Dock to secure the help of "a good, fast fish boat." The first skipper he approached turned him down, stating that "there are too many sheep

The worst day in California lighthouse history was April 5, 1951. This picture was taken just five minutes before the tragic loss of three lighthouse men. Left to right: Coast Guardsmen Vandenburg (standing by to unhook), Beckett (sitting on railing), Walker (securing life jacket), Costello, and Mulcahy (in stern). Only keepers Mulcahy and Vandenburg survived. (U.S. Coast Guard)

Here the crew is in the boat ready to be lowered. Moments later a sneaker wave capsized the boat and three fine men were lost. April 5, 1951. (U.S. Coast Guard)

out there." ("Sheep" are whitecaps.) Further down the dock, the Pilands found another commercial fishing vessel, the big drag boat *Winga*. With Donald Piland joining the *Winga*'s crew, the drag boat rushed off toward St. George Reef.

When the *Winga*'s crew arrived at St. George Reef, they found a terrible scene. Only Permenter and the two men at the buoy, Coast Guardsmen Mulcahy and Vandenberg, were conscious. Electrician's mate Beckett was unconscious, but alive. The other two men were dead. All the way back to Crescent City, Donald Piland worked ceaselessly, attempting to revive young Beckett. When the *Winga* arrived at Citizen's Dock, Wayne Piland had a doctor and an ambulance waiting. The doctor rushed to Coast Guardsman Beckett; then, sadly, pronounced him dead.

With three fine Coast Guardsmen dead, it was the worst tragedy in California lighthouse history. No other station had ever lost as many of its personnel at one time. In fact, only Año Nuevo Island had ever lost as many as two of its keepers at once. When combined with the two men who died in the light's early years, the deaths of the three Coast

Decommissioning ceremonies on May 13, 1975, last day of operation at St. George Reef. The colors come down for the final time. (Steven Yarbrough, Del Norte Triplicate)

Guardsmen brought the total number of lighthouse personnel lost to five. St. George Reef had proven to be the most deadly light station in the United States.

The next year, 1952, was another bad one at St. George Reef. A keeper suffered a mental breakdown; and Wayne Piland and Coast Guard officials had to land on the light and help remove him. Then, as if to underscore the hardship, the winter of 1952 was the worst in the reef's history. During one storm, waves at least one hundred sixty feet high swept over the top of St. George Reef lighthouse, shattering the windowpanes in the lantern room 146 feet above normal water.

Given such a harsh environment, the Coast Guard attempted to improve the safety at St. George Reef. Abandoning the light or automating it were both still out of the question. Limited space and high winds made using helicopters impractical. Thus, the lighthouse continued to be manned and serviced by ship. From now on, however, when men were taken on or off the reef, a Coast Guard cutter would be standing by to assist. The policy soon paid off. In 1958, while transferring personnel, the keepers' boat capsized, pitching four men into the water. The cutter *Ewing* was standing by, and it was only due to her commanding officer's alert action that the men were saved.

Eventually, even better methods evolved. After 1960, the 95-foot patrol boat *Cape Carter* was stationed at Crescent City. The *Cape Carter* was well suited for transferring people at St. George Reef. She would glide slowly in under the lighthouse boom until the ship was directly under the Billy Pugh net. As a swell carried the *Cape Carter* upward, three keepers would clamber into the net. While the patrol boat quickly backed away from the reef, the men in the net were hauled up to the lighthouse. A highly maneuverable 44-foot motor lifeboat stood by during the entire operation. Regularly dispatched to the reef from Chetco River Coast Guard Station (thirteen miles to the north in Oregon), the "44" could pluck a keeper from the water much faster than the larger *Cape Carter*. Additionally, anyone riding the Billy Pugh net was required to wear a wet suit as insulation against the cold water should an accident occur.

Sometimes the Coast Guard's big ocean-going tug *Comanche* serviced the lighthouse. The *Comanche*'s home port was Humboldt Bay; and when the tug took personnel off the reef the men were usually landed at Fields Landing near Eureka rather than at Crescent City. Larger vessels such as the *Comanche* or the buoy tender *Blackhaw* serviced St. George Reef when it was necessary to pump fresh water or fuel into the light station. The larger ships could not be worked in as close to the reef as could the *Cape Carter*, so it was necessary to put a small boat over the side and work it in under the net. The tug or buoy tender was secured to a mooring buoy during refueling operations and

The ancient Billy Pugh net is used for the last time as cutter Cape Carter's *crew grapple to hold net steady for an instant so that keepers can jump on board. May 13, 1975. (Steven Yarbrough,* Del Norte Triplicate*)*

personnel transfers. Only very calm days were chosen for pumping operations.

During the early 1970's, Kurt Neuharth served as assistant keeper. He provides us with an excellent description of daily life inside St. George Reef lighthouse as it existed during the last days of manned operation:

I get up at 6:30 and have breakfast between 6:45 and 7:30. At 7:30, I clean my room or any other area that has been assigned to me by the Officer-in-Charge. Then at 8:00 I start working: painting, repair, maintenance, and many other things. We work until 11:45, have lunch for an hour, then return to work until 4:00. Sometime during the (24) hour day each person has a radio watch. That is, he calls Humboldt Bay (Coast Guard Station) every hour. The radio contact is our only contact with the mainland, between the supply ship's run (which occurs once) every two weeks. (These hourly calls) serve as a safety measure. If we stopped calling them, they would know something is wrong and would send a boat out here to see what the trouble is.

At nights, we can watch television or listen to the radio. A person has to use his imagination to find things to do out here. Each one of us stays on the island for a duration of four weeks. Then he gets two weeks liberty ... off the island. He then comes back to the lighthouse for four more weeks.

This lighthouse was built in 1891 to point out to mariners the reef between the island and the mainland. The main device we use to point the reef out is the light atop the lighthouse. The light's rotating lens was built in 1890 in Paris. It has 225,000 candle power and can be seen from a distance of 18 miles. There are 12 sides to the rotating lens. Each side makes a complete rotation in one minute. The source of light is a 1,000-watt light bulb inside the lens.

We have a fog horn that is used when fog rolls in (and) ... visibility is down to five miles or less. We also have a radio beacon that planes and ships both use. This radio signal helps the vessels plot their course of travel.

There are generators that produce all the electricity we use. The ship that brings our supplies also brings our fuel and water for the generators. (The station storage tanks inside the base) can hold approximately 10,000 gallons of fuel and more than 50,000 gallons of water. This water also fills our everyday needs.

... we get on and off the island by using a "basket" (Billy Pugh net) lowered over the side of the lighthouse. A boat comes under the basket and we jump on it. The process is reversed when someone comes to the lighthouse. It always is an adventure when you have to use that thing, especially when the seas are rough and the ship is rocking wildly.

Christmas could be a particularly lonely time. The four-man crew sometimes had little more than a single, small chicken as the holiday entree. In a letter to the author's students, keeper Neuharth describes Christmas, 1973, on the reef:

When you're stationed on a lighthouse every letter received is a gift in itself.

The weather out here over the holidays was rather wet and cold. We made the best of the situation and had a Christmas tree and all the trimmings. Our wives and families sent us a number of surprise presents. So, over all, it was an enjoyable day. With the weather being so messy we didn't get a visit from the man

himself. I really don't think it would be a good idea to try and lift Mr. Claus in the Billy Pugh net anyway.

There was to be only one more Christmas at St. George Reef. By 1974 plans were well under way to abandon the light station and to moor a large navigational buoy nearby as a replacement. Such "super buoys" or "L.N.B.'s" feature a light, fog signal, and radio beacon and are so costly that they are normally only used to replace lightships. But landing is so difficult at St. George Reef that it would be the only lighthouse in the United States to be unmanned by using a large navigational buoy.

The final winter was typical. In February, 1975, officer-in-charge James W. Sebastian wrote:

This winter has been a long and lonely one. The weather does not always cooperate when it comes time to change crews and go home to families. We have spent many extra weeks on St. George due to high winds and rough seas. We hope it will soon be over.

It was. The big buoy was towed out and stationed nearby in April. Sebastian and his men spent several weeks watching the buoy to be certain it was operating reliably. Then, on May 13, 1975, the *Cape Carter* made the last run to remove the crew. The colors were lowered and, for the last time, the old derrick swung two men in the Billy Pugh net down onto the cutter's deck. Then, Chief Sebastian and Petty Officer Louis W. Salter chained the lighthouse door shut and motored out to the cutter in a rubber raft. The last human feet left at 12:10 p.m. The lighthouse was left completely intact, even the lens remaining in its time-honored position. America's greatest lighthouse was now dark.

Today, the lighthouse may be viewed from several places along the Del Norte County shore. The north side of Point St. George offers the best view, but many places along U.S. Highway 101 north of Crescent City provide good vantage points as the road skirts the the shore. A clear day and a good pair of binoculars provide the best results.

Perhaps someday a qualified boatman will initiate an excursion service to Northwest Seal Rock so that visitors can see the great sentinel close at hand. The summer months have many calm days when such a trip is quite feasible. Under no circumstances should visitors attempt a landing, however; nor should the trip be made except under the best weather conditions and, even then, only when employing a skilled pilot with good local knowledge. It is well to remember that while this beautiful granite tower is America's greatest lighthouse, it is also the nation's most dangerous as well.

St. George Reef lighthouse is dark today, but its unparalleled significance in American history is undiminished. Storm waves sweep the reef in this February, 1960 storm. (U.S. Coast Guard)

LANGUAGE OF THE LIGHT KEEPER AND SURFMAN
A GLOSSARY

Airways Beacon—A rotating, reflecting light similar to those used at some airports.

Balcony—The projecting walkway around a lantern room or watch room on a lighthouse. Nearly all lighthouses have one or two balconies. Sometimes called a gallery.

Ball—The chimney covering atop the lantern room roof.

Beach Cart—A cart used to carry the beach apparatus to a shipwreck. Beach apparatus included a Lyle gun, breeches buoy, lines, shovels, and the like.

Beach Patrol—Originally any patrol along the beach to search for wrecks or to warn vessels away from the shore by using flares. With the advent of World War II, the term came to be applied specifically to military patrols aimed at preventing sabotage and landing by enemy agents.

Bell House—The frame structure housing the fog bell and clockwork bell-striking apparatus (timer). It generally had an attached tower (called the bell tower) which held the weight used to power the clockwork drive.

Bilge Keel—A narrow ridge running the length of a lightship hull near the water line. Designed to lessen the vessel's rolling during heavy weather.

Breeches Buoy—A device used to carry people across impassable surf during evacuation from a shipwreck. It consists of a ring-shaped life preserver with a pair of oversized canvas pants attached to the ring. A line is shot from shore to ship and secured at both ends. The breeches buoy is then drawn across. The person to be rescued climbs into the life ring, putting his feet through the pants legs. He is then hauled ashore.

Buoy Tender—See lighthouse tender.

Diaphone Fog Horn—A fog signal consisting of a piston driven by compressed air.

Drop Tube or Weight Trunk—The hollow shaft down the center of most lighthouses in which travels the weight that causes the lens to rotate.

Faking Box—A wooden box in which a Lyle gun's shot line was coiled in layers around wooden pins. The pins were mounted on a removable frame. When the pins were removed, the line was free-standing, ready to be paid out without entanglement when fired by the Lyle gun.

Fixed Light—A steady, non-flashing beam.

Fog Bell—A bell used as a fog signal. See *Bell House*.

Fog Signal—A device at a station used to provide a loud, patterned sound during foggy weather to aid mariners in establishing their position or to warn them away from a danger. Often called "fog horns," a somewhat inaccurate term since whistles, bells, explosives, sirens, gongs, cannons, *et al.*, also have served as fog signals.

Fog Signal Station—A station with more or less the same collection of buildings as a light station except that there was no lighthouse; the fog signal served as the sole aid to navigation.

Hawse Pipe—The pipe-like opening at the bow of a lightship which holds the *mushroom anchor* and through which the anchor chain is run out.

Keeper—Usually the attendant at a light station. Also refers to the officer-in-charge of a life-saving station.

Lamp—The oil lighting apparatus inside a lens. Early lamps usually had several circular wicks and had to be trimmed and fed several times a night. Glass chimneys were placed over the flame, both to increase brightness and to direct smoke up to a lure and out of the lantern room.

Lantern Room—The glassed-in room at the top of a lighthouse containing the lens.

Lead Line—A rope with an attached lead weight used to determine the ocean's depth.

Lens Apron—A full-length linen apron worn by early-day keepers while working in the *lantern room*. Lens aprons prevented lint and dust off the keeper's clothing from coming into contact with the lens.

Lens Lantern—Large lantern, occasionally mounted outside a building at a light station to serve as the light. Unlike lenses, which were housed in a lantern room, lens lanterns were self-contained and were placed outside buildings. Lens lanterns were also commonly used on *lightships*.

Life Car—A small, submarine-like boat completely sheathed in metal and having a small hatch for entry. Designed to pass through surf too high to allow use of a *breeches buoy*, it could be drawn between ship and shore in much the same manner.

Lifeboat—In the U.S. Life-Saving Service, a self-bailing and self-righting pulling boat with air compartments. Manned by six oarsmen and a coxswain who used a steering oar. Lifeboats were heavier and larger than *surfboats* and were generally launched from a launchways or cart rather than by hand.

Lifeboat Station—A Coast Guard station equipped with primarily motor lifeboats. Originally, nearly all such stations had 36-foot motor lifeboats which were launched from marine railways.

Life-Saving Station—Established by the U.S. Life-Saving Service, most such stations were equipped with pulling (oar-powered) *lifeboats* and *surfboats*, which were launched through the surf by hand or by using a specially designed wagon called a *boat carriage*. These stations usually lacked launchways since they were frequently located on beaches having heavy breakers which would have destroyed a marine railway.

Light Station—Refers not only to the lighthouse, but to all of the buildings at an installation having a lighthouse. Light stations often had a fog signal building, oil house, carpenter shop, blacksmith shop, cistern, water house, laundry shed, *et al.*, in addition to the lighthouse itself. Some light stations have had more than one lighthouse.

Lighthouse Tender—Small ship used to supply light and fog signal stations, maintain buoys, and service lightships. Today, similar vessels are called *buoy tenders*.

Lightship—A moored vessel which marks a harbor entrance or a danger such as a reef. Lightships are usually equipped with a light, fog signal, and radio beacon. They are generally painted red with large, white lettering proclaiming the location they mark, e.g., Blunts Reef, Columbia River, or San Francisco. When the regular lightship returns to port for maintenance, a lightship marked *Relief* replaces it.

Lure—A large, inverted funnel in a lantern room which trapped smoke from the *lamp* and directed it up the chimney to escape via the *ball* atop the roof.

Lyle Gun—A small cannon used to shoot an 18-pound weighted projectile, with a line attached, from shore to a shipwreck.

Motor Lifeboat—A self-bailing and self-righting powered lifeboat designed to operate in heavy surf. In the U.S. Coast Guard, such boats are 36, 44, or 52 feet in length and are called for duty under the most extreme sea conditions.

Mushroom Anchor—A large anchor shaped like a mushroom and used on almost all modern Coast Guard lightships.

Oil House—A small building, usually of concrete or stone, used to store oil for the lighthouse lamps. Oil houses were built after kerosene came into use as an illuminant. Kerosene was so flammable that it could no longer be stored in or immediately adjacent to the lighthouse as had been the practice with less dangerous oils.

Patrol Boat—A Coast Guard rescue boat, usually of 82 to 95 feet in length, frequently used for such duties as searching for missing vessels, towing disabled craft, and transferring personnel at offshore light stations.

Radio Beacon—A radio-sending device which transmits a coded signal by which a mariner can determine his position using his own radio-direction-finding apparatus.

Sandpounder—Slang term for early beach patrolmen who walked their patrols.

Shot—A measurement of anchor chain length. One shot equals 90 feet.

Siren—A fog signal in which steam or compressed air is forced through slots in a rapidly spinning disk, thus producing a loud noise.

Surfboat—In the U.S. Life-Saving Service, a clinker-built pulling boat designed for use in heavy surf. Surfboats had to be lightweight so as to be launched by hand from remote beaches.

Surfman—The Life-Saving Service crew who manned the pulling boats, stood lookout duty, and walked the beach patrols. Most life-saving stations had six to eight surfmen in the crew, all under the command of a station keeper.

Vertical Mushroom Trumpet Fog Horns—A fog horn mounted vertically with a mushroom-shaped cover which directs the sound horizontally in all directions. Used on lightships and on offshore stations where the sound signal must be heard in all directions. In contrast, shore stations usually have horizontally mounted horns pointing in one or two directions away from shore.

Watch Room—The room where a light keeper stood watch. In a lighthouse, the watch room was usually either directly beneath the lantern room or beside the tower entrance. Fog signal buildings often had watch rooms as well.

Whistle—A fog signal through which steam or compressed air was forced. Fog whistles are classified by their diameter, i.e., a 12-inch whistle is 12 inches in diameter.

Wickie—Term for a light keeper, originating in the recurrent task of trimming the wicks.

ACKNOWLEDGMENTS

It was because the following people kindly gave of their time that this book could be written. Each person's knowledge and encouragement served as the building blocks that helped create this book. Either in their memories or their manuscripts, they have preserved the history of the Redwood Coast.

U.S. Lighthouse Service: Bill and Isabel Owens; Wayne and Martha Piland and daughter, Nancy; Harry Miller; J. Milford and Louise Johnson; Stephen Pozanac; Mrs. Esther Gonzales; Earl F. Mayeau; Mr. and Mrs. Charles Zetterquist; The Rev. James Otter; Ole and Bernice Lunden.

U.S. Life-Saving Service and U.S. Coast Guard: Cornelius Sullivan; Carl Christensen; Garner and Thora Churchill; Howard Underhill; Samuel "Hank" Mostovoy; Harry Hoffman; John Cathers; David Kissling; Bob Moore; Kurt Neuharth; Tom Smith; Gerald "Andy" Anderson; Nancy Bell; Jack Dusch; Dale Matlock; Ted Nutting; Brent Franze; Mark Dobney. And the officers and crews of *San Francisco Lightship, Number 100* and *Columbia River Lightship, WLV 604* and the Coast Guard cutters *Cape Carter, Modoc,* and *Point Barrow.*

U.S. Coast Guard, Aids to Navigation Office, 12th District: especially O. F. "Ollie" De Graaf, Commander J. S. Blackett, and Mrs. Anita Hale. (This office's files contain the nation's best material on California lighthouses and are an indispensable source for serious researchers. It is located at 630 Sansome Street in San Francisco.)

U.S. Coast Guard Public Affairs, 12th District: especially Paul Mobley and Jerry Cross.

U.S. Bureau of Land Management, Ukiah.

California State Library, Sacramento.

Clarke Museum, Eureka.

Del Norte County Historical Society; especially Helen Williams.

Humboldt State University Library: especially Eric Shimps.

Mendocino County Historical Society: especially Julia Moungovan and Robert Lee.

National Archives, Washington, D.C. and San Bruno, California: especially Robyn D. Gottfried.

Point Reyes National Seashore: especially Diana Skyles.

Public Libraries of Eureka, Garberville, Marin County, and San Francisco.

San Francisco Maritime Museum: especially David Hull and Richard Griffith.

We would also like to thank the following individuals: Andrew Genzoli; Carla Ehat; James Hogg; Tony Macchi; Wallace Martin; Ruth Williamson; Steven Yarbrough; Ralph Hunter; Ralph and Viola Shanks, Sr.

The kindnesses extended by numerous other individuals and institutions are also gratefully appreciated.

BIBLIOGRAPHY

Adamson, H. C., *Keepers of the Lights* (New York: Greenberg, 1955).

Bingham, Helen, *In Tamal Land* (San Francisco: Calkins Publishing House, 1906).

Binns, Archie, *Lightship* (Portland: Binfords & Mort, 1934). A fictional work, but one which well illustrates life on an early West Coast lightship.

Buckmaster, Russell, "Centurial Beacon," *Pacifica Magazine* (Arcata, California, vol. 1, no. 7, December, 1971). Trinidad Head.

Carse, Robert, *Keepers of the Lights* (New York: Scribner, 1969).

Carter, George Goldsmith, *Looming Lights* (London: Readers Union and Constable, 1947).
, *The Goodwin Sands* (London: Constable, 1953).

Conklin, Irving D., *Guideposts of the Sea* (New York, 1939).

Del Norte Triplicate, *Bicentennial Edition* (Crescent City, California, 1976). Contains numerous articles on local maritime history.

Edwards, E. Price, *Our Seamarks* (London: Longmans Green, 1884).

Giambarba, Paul, *Surfmen and Lifesavers* (Centerville, Massachusetts: The Scrimshaw Press, 1967).

Gibbs, James A., *Sentinels of the North Pacific* (Portland: Binfords & Mort, 1955).
, *Shipwrecks of the Pacific Coast* (Portland: Binfords & Mort, 1971).
, *West Coast Lighthouses* (Seattle: Superior, 1974).

Harkins, Philip, *Coast Guard Ahoy* (New York: Harcourt Brace, 1943).

Holland, Francis Ross, Jr., *America's Lighthouses* (Brattleboro, Vermont: Stephen Green Press, 1972).

Hoover, Mildred Brooke, *The Farallon Islands* (Stanford, California: Stanford University Press, 1932).

Hussey, John A., ed., *Early West Coast Lighthouses* (San Francisco: The Book Club of California, 1964).

Hurd, Edith Thacher, *The Faraway Christmas: A Story of the Farallon Islands* (New York: Lothrop, Lee and Shepard, 1958).

Jackson, Walter A., *The Doghole Schooners* (Volcano, California: California Traveler, Inc., 1969).

Mason, Jack, *Point Reyes: The Solemn Land* (Inverness, California: North Shore Books, 1972).
, *Last Stage for Bolinas* (Inverness, California: North Shore Books, 1973).
, ed., *Point Reyes Historian* (Inverness, California), vol. I, no. 1 (Spring, 1977) and vol. II, no. 2 (Fall, 1977).

Morgan, Judith and Neil Morgan, "Redwoods, Rain, and Lots of Room," *National Geographic*, vol. 152, no. 3, September, 1977.

Mueller, Richard, "Life on a Red Rubber Duck," *Pacifica Magazine* (Arcata, California, vol. 2, no. 1, June, 1972).

Nicholls, Joanna R., "The Life-Saving Service," *Frank Leslie's Popular Monthly*, vol. 43, no. 4, 1897.

Noble, Dennis L., *United States Life-Saving Service: Annotated Bibliography* (U.S. Coast Guard Headquarters, G-APA/83, Washington, D.C.).

O'Brien, T. Michael, *Guardians of the Eighth Sea: A History of the U.S. Coast Guard on the Great Lakes* (Cleveland: U.S. Coast Guard, 1976).

Plank, Robert, "Challenge of a Desolate Coast," *Pacifica Magazine* (Arcata, California, vol. 2, no. 1, June, 1972).

Putnam, George R., "Beacons of the Sea," *National Geographic*, vol. 24, no. 1, January, 1913.

    , *Lighthouses and Lightships of the United States* (Boston: Houghton Mifflin, 1917).

    , "New Safeguards for Ships in Fog and Storm," *National Geographic*, August, 1936.

    , *Sentinel of the Coasts: The Log of a Lighthouse Engineer* (New York: W. W. Norton, 1937).

Redwood Record, *The Trail Back: 100 Years in Southern Humboldt and Northern Mendocino Counties* (Garberville, California, 1974).
    Excellent material on Shelter Cove region.

Richardson, E. M., *We Keep a Light* (Toronto: The Ryerson Press, 1946).

Shanks, Ralph C., Jr. and Janetta Thompson Shanks, *Lighthouses of San Francisco Bay* (San Anselmo, California: Costaño Books, 1976).

Shanks, Ralph C., Jr., "Lighthouses of Marin," *Old Marin with Love* (San Rafael, California: Marin County American Revolution Bicentennial Commission, 1976).

    "The United States Life-Saving Service in California," *Sea Letter* (San Francisco: San Francisco Maritime Museum, No. 27, Spring, 1977).

Smith, Esther Ruth, *The First Crescent City Lighthouse* (Crescent City, California: Del Norte Historical Society), reprinted from *California Historical Society Quarterly*, vol. 35, no. 4, December, 1956.

Snow, Edward Rowe, *Famous Lighthouses of America* (New York: Dodd, Mead & Co., 1955).

Stevenson, D. Alan, *The World's Lighthouses Before 1820* (London: Oxford, 1959).

U.S. Coast Guard, *Aids to Navigation Manual* (CG222, various dates).

    , *The Coast Guardsman's Manual* (Annapolis: U.S. Naval Institute, 1967).

    , *Historically Famous Lighthouses* (Washington, D.C.: G.P.O., 1972).

    , *Light List, Pacific Coast and Pacific Islands* (Washington, D.C.: G.P.O., various years).

    , "Notice to Mariners" (12th and 13th Coast Guard Districts, San Francisco and Seattle, various dates).

U.S. Department of Commerce, *United States Coast Pilot, Pacific Coast* (Washington, D.C.: G.P.O., various years).

U.S. Life-Saving Service, *Annual Reports* (Washington, D.C.: G.P.O., 1878-1914).

Weiss, George, *The Lighthouse Service* (New York: AMS Press, reprinted 1974. Originally published 1926).

ABOUT THE AUTHORS

Ralph and Janetta Shanks are also the authors of *Lighthouses of San Francisco Bay.* They have taught courses on lighthouse history at the College of Marin and in the public schools. Mr. Shanks has written on the U.S. Life-Saving Service for the San Francisco Maritime Museum *Sea Letter.* He has also served as a consultant on the history and preservation of lighthouses and lifeboat stations for the U.S. Coast Guard, the Bureau of Land Management, and the National Park Service. Along with their young daughters, Torrey and Laurel, the Shanks are long-time residents of the Redwood Coast.